MASTERS AT WORK

MASTERS AT WORK

BECOMING
A PRIVATE
INVESTIGATOR

HOWIE KAHN

SIMON & SCHUSTER

New York   London   Toronto   Sydney   New Delhi

Simon & Schuster
1230 Avenue of the Americas
New York, NY 10020

Copyright © 2019 by Simon & Schuster, Inc.

First Simon & Schuster hardcover edition May 2019

SIMON & SCHUSTER and colophon are registered trademarks
of Simon & Schuster, Inc.

For information about special discounts for bulk purchases,
please contact Simon & Schuster Special Sales at 1-866-506-1949
or business@simonandschuster.com.

The Simon & Schuster Speakers Bureau can bring authors to your
live event. For more information or to book an event, contact the
Simon & Schuster Speakers Bureau at 1-866-248-3049
or visit our website at www.simonspeakers.com.

Interior design by Jennifer K. Beal Davis

Manufactured in the United States of America

1   3   5   7   9   10   8   6   4   2

Library of Congress Cataloging-in-Publication Data

Names: Kahn, Howie, author.
Title: Becoming a private investigator / Howie Kahn.
Description: New York : Simon & Schuster, 2019. | Series: Masters at work
Identifiers: LCCN 2018057870| ISBN 9781982103989 (hardcover) | ISBN
9781982103996 (ebook)
Subjects: LCSH: Private investigators. | Private security
services—Vocational guidance.
Classification: LCC HV8081.K34 2019 | DDC 363.28/9023—dc23
LC record available at https://urldefense.proofpoint.com/v2
/url?u=https-3A__lccn.loc.gov_2018057870&d=DwIFAg&c=jGUuvAd
BXp_VqQ6t0yah2g&r=jOP_-CgRZWvBrDdCwa8xatiC6xfq_b-txHvQ
-EzzwapJfII4Aa7gU5HEQRlR4PPw&m=Xl-p5qcrqrpjgVxalrVVSN6k
TUOwteuSIhyhJ9dOg60&s=h2pUHlXEXko5SWHNJCf24raT_
-YvW1_zQoSu8MbaZQc&e=

ISBN 978-1-9821-0398-9
ISBN 978-1-9821-0399-6 (ebook)

AUTHOR'S NOTE

Certain names and identifying facts have been altered by the author.

CONTENTS

BECOMING
A PRIVATE
INVESTIGATOR
─────────

INTRODUCTION

This is a book about real-life haunting. The private investigators chronicled are the ones who choose to take it on, working on behalf of the dead. Each of the deceased was laid to rest, but without peace. Their families and friends remained. Believing they'd been forsaken by law enforcement, they all sought help at the fringe of the law.

Not all private investigators focus on the dead. Some make a living busting cheating spouses for fees ranging from $50 per hour on the lower end to $500,000 for a longer-lasting, high society sting. Other PIs work on contract for insurance providers, investigating claims ranging from alleged on-the-job injuries to property and vehicle damage.

Fortune 500 caliber companies hire PIs to conduct background checks on potential employees, to look into current employees suspected of wrongdoing, and to make sure disgruntled ex-employees don't return to their erstwhile offices with a gun and the intentions to use it. Increasingly, wealthy parents are hiring private investigators to deliver intelligence to them on their sons' or daughters' significant others in order to avoid bringing a fraud or a grifter into the family fold. Other parents need private investigators to help them find their missing or kidnapped children. Those cases can last hours, weeks, or years.

According to the US Department of Labor's Bureau of Labor Statistics, 41,400 private investigators were working in the US in 2016 with a projected occupational growth rate of 11 percent by 2026. Seven percent is the average occupational growth rate for jobs here, so the number of PIs in America, according to the BLS, is growing "faster than average." That may be because of the dying nature of privacy itself. As social media has made it easier than ever to take account of the lives of others, more people spend at least some part of their day investigating somebody else in a casual way. A desire to professionalize that behavior with greater frequency seems inevitable in our burgeoning surveillance society; Facebook stalking can easily be an antecedent to a career in computer forensics. Start-up culture, hinged on the notion of disrupting institutional norms, may also contribute to the growth of the private investigation field. Since the criminal justice system does not always perform with the greatest amount of precision, PIs can often fill in and expose staggering investigative gaps thereby acting as disruptors. According to the Murder Accountability Project, a nonprofit founded in 2015 by a retired investigative reporter turned homicide archivist named Thomas K. Hargrove, there have been more than 200,000 unsolved murders in the United States since 1980.

In talking with more than a dozen private investigators, each one emphasized rehabilitating the image of their profession. There's concern, industry-wide, that there's too much confusion between their actual work and that belonging to hard-boiled detective characters from TV, on film, and in literature. Being a PI has nothing to do, one investigator told me, "with a pebbled glass door and a leggy secretary."

News headlines can also cast PIs as morally dubious bottom-feeders doing the dirty work for the wealthy. In 2006, Anthony Pellicano, a famous Hollywood PI, was indicted on 110 counts, including charges of racketeering, conspiracy, wiretapping, and identity theft. Ultimately sentenced to fifteen years in federal prison, Pellicano is scheduled for release in March 2019.

Even more recently, it was reported that disgraced (and disgraceful) film executive Harvey Weinstein hired PIs from Black Cube (a firm led by former Israeli intelligence officials) to assume false identities and probe and gather information on the women who would go on to publically accuse of him of an array sex crimes, leading to a June 2019 trial.

Even the history of the profession is steeped in stories of PIs working beyond the pale, seeking justice, but flexible and conditional about the definition of the term. The first PI is largely said to be Eugène François Vidocq, a Frenchman who lived from 1775 to 1857. From age thirteen, Vidocq was a thief and a prisoner, a performer in a troupe of traveling entertainers, an active soldier, and a military deserter. At twenty, he went back to prison, escaped several times, and had his sentence extended for forging a prison pardon. More arrests and escapes followed for the next decade. But at thirty-four, Vidocq chose to become an informant for the police and eventually parlayed that job into starting what became the investigative wing of the Paris police department. In his late fifties, Vidocq founded *Le Bureau des Renseignements* in 1833, a private detective agency with almost a dozen detectives on staff. His agency and the police quarreled constantly over money, power, influence, and the legality of his work. They raided his office and arrested him on several occasions, charging him with deception, corruption, and financial crimes.

The United States' first famous private investigator, Allan Pinkerton, a Scottish-born barrel maker whose Illinois home was a stop on the Underground Railroad, founded his agency, first called the North-Western Police Agency and, later, the Pinkerton National Detective Agency, in 1850. During the Civil War, Pinkerton was said to have once saved Abraham Lincoln from assassination. Later, Pinkerton specialized in railway security and was hired to track down Jesse James and put an end to his criminal outfit, the James Gang. The pursuit was relentless, but ultimately a failure. After Pinkerton's death, his agency took on corporate clients who hired them to bust up fledgling labor unions. According to the Pinkertons' time line, the company is also responsible for hiring the United States' first female PI, Kate Warne, in 1856, establishing the country's first criminal database, and disbanding Butch Cassidy and the Wild Bunch. In 1999, Pinkerton's was bought by Securitas AB, the Swedish global security giant, for almost $400 million.

"This is a real profession now, with real money at stake," one investigator told me. "It's legitimate, like being a lawyer or being an accountant." An increasing number of high-profile stories show PIs working to unravel issues of global and political consequence. Christopher Steele, a former spy for MI6, the British Secret Intelligence Service, and co-founder of Orbis Business Intelligence, a private investigation agency, was paid $168,000 to do opposition research on then US presidential candidate Donald Trump.

Steele's work on the case resulted in a dossier alleging close ties between Trump and Russia, helping to launch the current federal investigation led here by the special counsel, Robert Mueller.

Elsewhere in the UK, Bellingcat, who bills itself as a kind of private investigation-journalism hybrid project, led by a thirty-nine-year-old blogger named Eliot Higgins, has been working publically to out a group of Russian men believed to have poisoned former Russian spy Sergei Skripal and his daughter, Yulia, in Salisbury, England, in March 2018. "States are increasingly losing their monopoly over spying," Jonathan Eyal, a global security expert and the associate director of Royal United Services Institute, who trains governments and big businesses to protect themselves, told the *New York Times*. "Now it belongs to anyone who has the brains, the spunk and the technological ability."

Gumption, tech savvy, and a high IQ aren't the only credentials needed to become a wave-making PI. Private investigators have rules to follow and standards to meet. For the most part in America, states set the guidelines for who can be a PI and who cannot. Forty-five of our states have statewide licensing requirements. Idaho, Mississippi, and South Dakota all have private professional associations for PIs with their own bylaws. The Alaskan cities of Anchorage and Fairbanks have city-mandated requirements for PIs as does the city of Cheyenne, Wyoming, where statewide licensing doesn't exist.

There are no federal regulations as to who gets licensed, though certain states do send candidate's background information and/or fingerprints to the FBI for analysis. Studying criminal justice for a formal degree or certificate program can help a new PI break into the fold; years spent working in a related field can be counted toward a license.

As a licensed PI, the scope of available work is immediately huge. Broadly, the job permits you to investigate pretty much anything on behalf of a client (within the scope of legal behavior). That may mean tracking down a serial killer or a fraud. It may mean conducting background checks on search engines not accessible to the public, or surveilling cheaters, kidnappers, people running for office, or candidates for high-profile jobs. Collecting accurate, relevant information is the aim. While writing this book, a number of PIs expressed their belief to me that there are no real secrets anymore. There's only the time it takes to pry lips and information loose.

Plenty of PIs are former cops, but plenty of PIs also believe they have jobs because of what cops and other law enforcement agents can, and do, miss in their investigations. Cases stall out or go cold for many reasons. Sometimes, a police department doesn't have the man power or budgetary resources to sustain a long-term investigation. Sometimes, they botch a crime scene so badly that they bury the case to make their own mistakes disappear from public view. And sometimes, there's a strong whiff of foul play: corruption, collusion, cops, lawyers, and judges conducting illegal business of their own.

The PIs in this book believe justice isn't a given. Justice is the result of tenacity, pressuring public officials, continuous public outrage, and asking the right sources the right questions at exactly the right time. Collectively, these PIs also believe that they're the last line of defense for the vulnerable. "You don't go to a private investigator like you go to a florist," one prominent PI told me. "People call us because they're in a terrible place."

Tellingly, the cases in this book come from the worst places: the living trying to make sense of somebody they love dying suddenly and violently. For those grieving—for months and years—law enforcement didn't cut it. No satisfactory conclusions were reached by them. Calling on private investigators meant sustaining a posture of hope: there were answers to find and a PI, the right PI, might be the only person to find them. Unlike cops or feds who will ultimately have to move on to other cases, PIs can work a single case for as long they agree to and for as long as their clients remain satisfied with their efforts. The best PIs take on their clients' ghosts as their own.

The investigations that follow are yearslong; some, still ongoing. I chose to discuss some cases without conclusions because they best illuminate the most grueling elements of the job. Where so many of today's careers demand lightning-fast results and daily proof of bulk achievement, private investigation can often move at a bygone pace. PIs must routinely be patient and careful. They know how to wait and know just when to strike.

It's the most difficult cases that represent the highest virtues of the job: the balance between tenacity and empathy, the way a broken heart can be an investigation's propellant rather than its deterrent.

The vast majority of the case information in these pages come from the rigorous investigative work conducted by the PIs themselves. Their cases yielded hundreds of pages of interviews, based on hundreds of hours of talking and developing sources. Reports and affidavits are critical as are grisly crime-scene and autopsy photos, computer-animated recreations of events, 911 call recordings, subpoenaed text and Facebook messages, and scientific reports examining everything—from blood alcohol levels to which way a body might float if lifeless in a certain part of a specific lake in the middle of Tennessee. It all reads like a story, but it's really the evidence they've collected, the documents they've assembled, and the conclusions they're nearing, still working toward, or have reached.

The rigor shown by these PIs is matched only by their moral focus. They see themselves as the only bridge remaining to the truth.

1

Sheila Wysocki wants to send me back home to New York City with a sandwich. We're eating lunch at a place called the Puffy Muffin, near her home in Nashville, Tennessee. It's a Tuesday in May. The place is packed, crowded with women: salon-fresh blondes in pastels, many of them on a first-name basis with the wait staff. Wysocki, fifty-five, does not lunch. "I don't get invited to the foofoo girl things," she says. She's wearing inconspicuous blues: jeans and a navy blouse. Her eyes are brown: expressive but not dramatic. Their lids will narrow to convey focus, concern, or empathy. Her hair is thick and dark, styled subtly, cut short in the back with bangs in the front. Wysocki lets out an exhale and says her work has left her sleepless for weeks: her blood pressure is dangerously high, her doctor is worried. He says she should consider taking a break, perhaps indefinitely. Earlier, at her house I saw an envelope on her desk addressed to "Sheila Wysocki Pit Bull P.I.!" Since

2004, she has spent her days and nights investigating cold case murders.

Wysocki, who calls herself "pushy," "nosey," and a "helicopter mom" (her sons are twenty-two and twenty-six; their father is her husband of thirty years) nods at the food remaining on our table. "Can I send this home to your wife?" she asks. "Take something with you." There's a refrigerated case near the Puffy Muffin's front door selling take-out pimento cheese and white cake with sprinkles in a cup. Toward the back of the restaurant are the rows of three-tiered Boston cream pies, each with their middle layer of pudding exposed like a midriff. Wysocki says she used to be the kind of parent who baked and participated in Christmas cookie exchanges. She calls what changed her course a "God Nod."

"I get a God Nod," a kind of spiritual prompt, "when I'm supposed to do things," Wysocki says. This particular, life-altering nod was telling her to figure out who raped and murdered her college roommate, Angela Samota. "You're picking the Puffy Muffin, of all places, to talk about Angie?" Wysocki says, lowering her chin.

It's Wysocki's operating theory that evil lurks in unexpected places and the bloodiest crimes happen in a flash.

Because she believes safety is transient, at best, she named her business Without Warning Private Investigation. Talking murder in the Puffy Muffin only serves to underscore her point.

In 1984, Wysocki—then Sheila Gibbons—was a twenty-two-year-old student studying psychology on scholarship at Southern Methodist University in Dallas. Since money was tight, she lived at home with her mother, Janis, about thirty minutes north of SMU. Early in the afternoon on Saturday, October 13, Wysocki was just getting back to her mom's from a haircut when the phone rang. It was Barbara Paschall, one of Angie's sorority sisters, breathlessly telling Wysocki that something horrible had happened overnight and that Angie was dead.

The rookie Dallas police officer assigned to the crime scene, Janice Crowther, then twenty years old, has said Angie's heart appeared to have been cut from her chest. She'd been stabbed eighteen times. The police report concluded that "vaginal intercourse occurred at or near the time of death."

Panicked, heartbroken, and in disbelief, Wysocki rushed back toward campus where friends of Angie's were holding vigil at the apartment of Angie's then boyfriend, a construction manager named Ben McCall. After that, Wysocki left SMU, never returning to the classes in which she'd enrolled. "I didn't feel safe there anymore," Wysocki recalls. "I couldn't go back."

Having dropped out of school, Wysocki started working with her mother full-time. They'd already been cleaning homes together around the Dallas area. Wysocki had been hired to clean for both Angie and Ben McCall. In addition to the housekeeping jobs, Wysocki joined her mother's catering company on weekends, working weddings and church events. But Wysocki was suffering. Her anxiety spiked. She remembers many nights sleeping on the floor next to her mother's bed, even though she was twenty.

She also began meeting with a Dallas Police detective, noirishly named Virgil Sparks, about Angie's case. Sparks showed Wysocki photographs from the crime scene: Angie's lifeless body surrounded by blood, her bright, blue eyes open and vacant, like a long-neglected doll's. Wysocki learned there were three suspects: an ex-boyfriend of Angie's who, according to the police report, had threatened her with a knife; her current boyfriend, Ben McCall, who reported to the police that something wasn't right after receiving a cryptic late-night telephone call from Angie; and Russell Buchanan, a twenty-three-year-old architect, who was part of the group Angie had gone out with the night she was killed.

The ex-boyfriend's alibi, that he was working in Amarillo, Texas, almost 400 miles away, quickly checked out and Sparks asked Wysocki if she could help him profile the two remaining persons of interest: McCall and Buchanan. As a peer, perhaps Wysocki could get information and gain trust in a way that a middle-aged cop could not. Wysocki agreed and after she started meeting with McCall and Buchanan, she would then meet up with Sparks at the bars of popular Dallas establishments like Snuffers or Cardinal Puffs where he would drink booze and she'd drink Diet Cokes while disclosing her findings.

Soon, scientific evidence would eliminate any suspicions about McCall. Police thought the way he reported what was then his suspicion of a disturbance sounded too cool and casual, as if he didn't really care. But, critically, he'd given police saliva samples that proved his blood secreted antigens into his bodily fluids. This critical fact meant that you could decipher his blood type from his spit. Police knew, however, that the person who raped and murdered Angie did not secrete blood antigens into their bodily fluids, proven from a semen swab taken at the crime scene. (This was 1984, and

DNA testing, which matches to a specific person and not the broader category of blood type, didn't start until 1985.)

Since Buchanan's saliva swab indicated that he was a nonsecretor—and perhaps *the* nonsecretor—he remained the only suspect. "They told me Russell killed Angie," Wysocki says. "They said the first kill is the hardest and that he'll do it again."

One night in 1985, at Sparks's behest, Wysocki arranged to have dinner with Buchanan. She was terrified, certain she was eating Chinese food with a murderer. He picked her up and, later, dropped her off. As she poked around for clues and did whatever amateur profiling she could, she wondered if a killer could also be such a nice guy. Later, Wysocki heard Buchanan hired the prominent Dallas criminal defense attorney Richard "Racehorse" Haynes, renowned for winning seemingly unwinnable murder trials for the accused. Hearing that, she became even more convinced of Buchanan's guilt. (Buchanan says this was all just a rumor and that the attorney he hired was named Reed Prospere.) But without substantial evidence, a case against Buchanan never materialized and he soon left the country for London. Wysocki figured he'd fled and had gotten away with murder.

Three years later, Wysocki was still talking to Sparks about the case. She got married that year, 1988, and invited the detective to her wedding, even though she was trying to move on with her life. She'd started a dress rental business, remembering the times at SMU when debutante functions would frequently require new evening wear, despite her having nowhere near the resources to have such a deep wardrobe. "We were extremely poor," Wysocki says. Her parents divorced when she was in high school. Wysocki's father was a traveling salesman and rarely around. Her mother began working after the divorce and put her cooking skills to use as a caterer and making meals in the executive dining room of an oil company. Wysocki called her dress rental business Lasting Impressions and added wedding dresses to her stock; her husband, Charles, she says, backed the endeavor and came up with the name. "That business was huge," she recalls, but she closed it in 1989 when her family moved to Tennessee for Charles's job.

Living outside of Nashville, Wysocki tried to put the memories of Angie Samota's murder behind her. She called Detective Sparks once in a while, but, otherwise, she raised her sons, flipped houses with her husband, an executive in the health care industry, and ran a spa. "That's the worst business ever," she says, citing both perpetual staffing issues and a general dissatisfaction with employees who seemed to only half-ass it. "I'm not real patient with people not show-ing up to work," Wysocki says. Charlie, her older son, is now an intellectual property attorney in Washington, DC, and Christopher, her youngest, is working toward a career in video game development. When Wysocki is approached by television producers who want to make shows about her life, they usually want to typecast her as a mother–private investigator hybrid, refusing to let one job be separate from the other. "One guy calls me," she says, "and he goes, 'Oh, after you solve the case, we can show you at the end of the night putting your children to bed!' And I said, 'Well, that's kind of creepy, my kids are twenty-two and twenty-five.'" Producers might have been wise to take a page from Wysocki's playbook before contacting her. "Get to know your subjects," she says. "I said to this guy, 'You know noth-ing about me, do you?'"

Three years before Wysocki became a PI, when Char-lie was about ten and Christopher was about six, they got sick from exposure to toxic black mold after a flood in the Wysocki's home. They had rashes, hair loss, migraines, and exhaustion. Christopher vomited blood. Charlie had a PICC line inserted to treat an infection. Diagnosing the problem became a full-time pursuit with Wysocki taking her kids to doctors all over the country to get them medically back on the right track. When I point out that she conducted a kind of investigation to get her kids the appropriate care, Wysocki does what she usually does when presented with a new theory. "That's an interesting way of seeing it," see says, neither accepting nor dismissing it, not assigning it value nor making it seem valueless. She files it away mentally and makes me feel heard.

"I was losing faith in the Catholic Church," Wysocki says. She'd been losing faith in Catholicism for a decade. It was now 2003. Her best friend had been murdered. Her children had been sick. Not wanting to veer into faithlessness, she started going to Bible study. "We had gotten the kids back into school and settled. My life had gone from hospitals and doctors' appointments and flying across the country to find the right people to treat my kids to suddenly having a lot of time on my hands." A friend invited Wysocki to join a Bible group for which they'd watch videos made by Beth Moore, the popular Houston-based founder of Living Proof Ministries, and then meet with other local women to drink iced tea, eat quiche, and discuss the week's passages. "At that time in my life," Wysocki says, "what else was I going to do?"

One night in 2004, Wysocki had gotten into bed with her homework: readings from the Book of Daniel. Wysocki had been through Daniel before. He was thrown in a furnace, but didn't burn. He was left with the lions, but didn't suffer a scratch. Daniel had visions: about the future of man and about eternal justice.

Wysocki, to her utter surprise, was about to have a vision, too. "I'm reading the Bible, I'm leaning back, I don't know if I was dozing, or awake, but I know what I saw." In front of her stood Angie Samota in apparition form, wearing items from her wardrobe that Wysocki recalled from their days at SMU: a brown argyle Ralph Lauren sweater with a matching skirt.

Having the vision, memories of her friend and details of the case came rushing back. Angie had been, by all accounts, brilliant. A computer science and electrical engineering major, and the social chair of her sorority, Angie had spent her last night alive with two friends, including Russell Buchanan, the young architect who would become the primary suspect in her death, and a classmate named Anita Kadala.

That night back in 1984, the three had tried to go for dinner at the chain restaurant Bennigan's, but left when it was too crowded. Dallas was bustling that weekend. The State Fair of Texas was in full swing and the number 1–ranked University of Texas football team was about to play out the seventy-ninth heated installment of their rivalry with the University of Oklahoma at the Cotton Bowl. Angie and her friends ultimately had dinner at a place called the Boardwalk Beach Club that boasted sandy floors and an indoor volleyball net. Then, they headed to Nostromos, a restaurant whose upstairs dance club, the Rio Room, was VIP only. They got in based on Angie's charisma and her connections. Around 1:00 a.m., they left and Angie dropped off her friends. She briefly stopped by Ben McCall's to say goodnight to her boyfriend. Less than two hours later, Angie was dead.

Twenty years later, in her bedroom in Nashville, Sheila Wysocki was seeing her former roommate just as she'd been: luminous, vivacious, and smiling. "I knew what it meant," Wysocki says. "It meant that it was time." It was time to find Angie's killer. It was time to fully honor the memory of her murdered friend. It was time to put Angie's family at ease with an arrest, a trial, and a conviction. Wysocki's "God Nod" delivered her a purpose and a mission. She put down her Bible, reached for her phone, and called the Dallas

Police Department. "That was the first time I was told they had lost all the evidence," Wysocki says.

When the police operator answered, Wysocki asked for the cold case division. She was told no such thing existed in Dallas, then the ninth largest city in the United States, and she was put through to homicide instead. She asked for the only cop she knew, Virgil Sparks, and says she left him fifty messages without receiving a call back. Wysocki kept on calling for months, and ultimately for years, hearing different stories from different members of the police force: the evidence was missing, they said. Later, they said it was lost in a flood.

For Wysocki, Angie's death left a series of psychological scars. No matter where she went, the feeling of threat remained pervasive. "I should have seen a therapist," Wysocki says. Still, she took other proactive measures. Wysocki trained in self-defense and learned to shoot a gun. She preferred to live in gated communities with staffed gatehouses and on cul-de-sacs, with a single, visible way in and way out. Wysocki requested that the guards patrol her suburban Nashville cul-de-sac on the regular and they'd stop and chat with her from time to time. She told them about Angie and about her vision of her. It's Nashville, she figured; nobody had a problem talking about ghosts.

Standing in her driveway, Wysocki revealed she'd been calling the Dallas Police Department and getting blown off, over and over. The head of neighborhood security, a fifty-one-year-old, six-foot-tall, 225-pound former police officer and bodyguard named J. D. Skinner had gotten to know Wysocki over the years. He was a principal at the security company (he'd later buy it) and, on top of neighborhood protection, it also had an investigative division.

After a few conversations, Skinner saw how closely "Ms. Wysocki," which he still calls her, paid attention to detail and how deeply she retained information. He knew she was relentless about protection and, in her way (which is present but noncombative), didn't back down from a challenge or a fight. So, Skinner had an idea.

"He told me to become a private investigator," Wysocki says. "He said he'd show me the ropes."

PI applicants in Tennessee must be over twenty-one, a US citizen or resident alien, and not declared incompetent due to "mental defect or disease" by a court (if such incompetence has been declared, but a court later rules for competence, you're back in the game). Candidates must not be alcoholics or drug addicts, though Wysocki says urine samples are not required, and, per the state, "must be of good moral character." When Wysocki applied for her PI license, she says letters of recommendation were submitted on her behalf. Their fingerprints are sent to both the FBI and TBI (Tennessee Bureau of Investigation).

According to the Tennessee Department of Commerce and Insurance, the body that regulates the private investigation industry within the state, candidates have to also be "affiliated with a licensed Tennessee Private Investigators Company." Skinner offered Wysocki a place within his company. But she would first have to pass a state-mandated exam, which Wysocki found problematic because she's dyslexic. "Reading and studying are the worst for me," she says. "Every time I even think about a test, the anxiety puts me over the edge. It doesn't matter what kind of test. A driver's test would do it."

If she passed, Wysocki would have the kind of license Skinner figured the Dallas police would take seriously. And, according to code, she'd have the authority to look into an array of offenses. Her employment, per the state of Tennessee, could involve tracking and learning about almost every aspect of a person's life, and she'd have the official capacity to seek the cause of "damages or injuries to persons" and to collect evidence for courts, boards, commissions, officers, or investigating committees. In short, if Wysocki could overcome the hurdle of the examination, she figured she'd be credentialed to solve Angie's murder.

Wysocki passed the 100-question exam after some unconventional test prep that involved her then thirteen-year-old son reading the recommended study materials to her out loud. Spoken information was more easily digested, whereas reading densely written, unfamiliar legal texts triggered Wysocki's dyslexia.

Nevertheless, even with her license, Wysocki says the detectives in Dallas started referring to her as a PITA rather than as a PI.

The letters, she says, laughing, were an acronym for "Pain In The Ass."

Still, licensing emboldened Wysocki and she started learning how to do her new job. She spoke more frequently with Skinner and her neighborhood security patrol. She began learning surveillance. While she found the hours of sitting and blending in time consuming and boring, developing interview techniques proved intriguing as Wysocki came face-to-face with people from all walks of life: Cops, businesspeople, even a stripper who had hired Wysocki to watch one of her patrons, hoping to glean when he might finally leave his wife, as promised, for his exotic dancer.

"Playing it dumb and nice started working for me," Wysocki says. She also started learning to use the search engines available to licensed investigators like TLO, the final company founded by the Florida entrepreneur Hank Asher, godfather of the data fusion business, for which computer software began merging thousands of existing databases at high speeds, giving people unparalleled, fast access to many of the puzzle pieces—social security numbers, addresses, asset location, arrest records—that tell the story of a human life (TLO stands for "The Last One," in reference to it being Asher's last launch). Wysocki learned to use other databases like Tracers and IRB later.

Investigative work, Wysocki discovered, could be more effective as a collaboration. For Angie's case, in 2005, she enlisted a friend who formerly worked for the FBI to comb through electronic databases that were even more obscure than the ones she was mastering. PIs also now make sure they can access the dark web. Greg Shaffer, a Dallas-based security services ace and private investigator with twenty years experience as an FBI agent, says he frequently contracts former NSA and CIA professionals, who have become certified ethical hackers, to tap into the dark web and look for hidden information about a suspect.

Aside from making phone calls to the Dallas police and performing database searches on anybody who might have known Angie Samota in the years leading up to her murder, Wysocki also began research on all unsolved murders in the Dallas area starting around the time of Angie's in 1984 and ranging through the next two decades. She wanted to know which ones also involved forced entry, which involved assault, which included stabbing, and which were coupled with rape. Maybe she'd spot a pattern, she thought. Maybe she'd deduce something that others had not by looking more closely, by spending more hours, by concentrating fully.

"I looked at everything," Wysocki says. She also pushed back against older findings. Did Angie's ex-boyfriend's alibi really check out? Could a fellow SMU student named Patrick, who was infatuated with Angie, have had anything to do with it? Wysocki knew Angie had traveled to Mexico in the months prior to her murder. "Could it have been the cartels?" Wysocki wondered. "Some of my thinking was crazy," she admits. But thoroughness was important, even taken to the extreme.

Since the cops had let the case go cold, Wysocki would try and put some heat on it by presenting new information. Her most reliable and results-generating investigative tool, however, turned out to be her persistence. Wysocki says she made over 700 calls to the Dallas Police Department. Her reasons for such strategic pestering were twofold. First, she knew nobody was calling about Angie at all except for her, and she wanted to constantly remind the cops that the case remained unsolved. Her calls were a pressure tactic; low pressure, perhaps, but repetitive communication, Wysocki felt, would at least keep Angie's name current. "Most people would have just stopped calling," she says. "The police were basically telling me to stop."

Wysocki's second reason for calling so much was that she could garner fragments of new information depending on who at DPD was tasked with answering her call. Part of Wysocki's investigation, in a sense, was to investigate the police—who knew what? When might the story of the evidence change as it had changed before? Wysocki intuited that they knew something, that the information was somewhere. Angie's records weren't lost to a flood, she thought. They were lost to a combination of bureaucratic disarray, institutional sluggishness, and human laziness. Or, nothing had been lost at all. The police had nothing to gain from admitting the information existed: they hadn't solved the case. They hadn't brought about justice. Lying about the files' whereabouts could have simply been a way of stalling until something could be done—or until Wysocki gave up.

In 2008, the Dallas Police Department launched a cold case division and by then DNA testing, which was not available in 1984, had become a trusted source of information in murder cases. Wysocki knew what samples were taken at the crime scene; she had the police report in her possession. Vaginal, oral, and anal swabs and smears had been collected in Angie's bedroom; a rape kit was administered; scrapings from beneath her fingernails were preserved. If any of that evidence survived at all, Angie's case could be solved by matching DNA to her perpetrator's.

One day in the fall of that year, Wysocki received a telephone call from a detective named Linda Crum, part of the new four-person cold case division at the Dallas Police Department. Wysocki's years of drum banging, perhaps, had made Angie's case one of the first on Crum's desk. When Crum told Wysocki that she had Angie's file and had ordered the case's evidence out from storage, Wysocki paused, thinking, she *has* a file? She *ordered* the evidence? After years of trying to make it happen, Wysocki knew the police were about to properly work on Angie's case.

When the DNA results came back, Wysocki was certain

they'd finally confirm what she'd been led to believe for al-most twenty-five years: that Russell Buchanan, by then a renowned architect in the Dallas area, had gone to Angie's apartment after she had dropped him off, entered angrily, and murdered her after she turned down his sexual ad-vances. But Linda Crum, who had called to tell Wysocki, "We got him," presented the private investigator with a dif-ferent name entirely.

After running the DNA through a database of criminal offenders, Crum found out that it matched the genetic in-formation of a sixty-year-old convicted felon named Donald Bess. Six feet tall and weighing more than 360 pounds, Bess was out on parole when Angie Samota was raped and mur-dered on October 13, 1984.

Six years earlier, in 1978, Bess had been given two 25-year sentences for separate incidents of aggravated rape and aggravated kidnapping, but he only served six years of that sentence before being released in what amounts to a tragic error in judgment. After being paroled in March of 1984, and getting away with Angie's murder seven months later, Bess was given a life sentence for a subsequent sexual assault in 1985. After Crum had the DNA evidence in hand, Bess was pulled from prison to stand trial for Angie's murder in

2010. He was sentenced to death and remains on death row, where Wysocki, through investigative sources she won't reveal, keeps tabs on him. He had a heart attack during the trial that delayed it for a couple days and she knows his cardiac problems persist. She also knows that he gets frequent mail from female admirers. Wysocki figures Bess will die of natural causes before his sentence is carried out. "God will get to it before the state does," is how Wysocki envisions Bess's ultimate fate.

As an investigator, Wysocki learned a cornerstone lesson from Angie's case: conclusive physical evidence is paramount; theories remain theories in the absence of proof. For decades, Wysocki had held onto the belief that Russell Buchanan had killed Angie Samota because she implicitly believed what the detectives had told her back in the 1980s. Brought up as a law-abiding, white Texas youth, Wysocki was taught to trust the cops. Questioning them wasn't polite; she took their word as gospel. When they told her Buchanan was unmarried and lived with his mother, she believed it; the description, she figured (despite living with her own mother) made sense and fit the profile of a killer. It turn out that "he's married," Wysocki says. "His wife is amazing."

In subsequent years, Wysocki says, she has learned more about the profile of killers and serial killers. "Hatred for women, mommy issues, white males with a history of violence," Wysocki says. "Intelligence is a marker, too."

Other details surrounding Angie's case, Wysocki had taken at face value: she had been told Buchanan had failed a polygraph, but he had not. It had also been believed that Buchanan's London trip was taken to make a getaway from the crime, but, in reality, she says, it was for graduate school.

After the trial, Buchanan saw Wysocki's strength and resiliency as a kind of silver lining. "She cleared everything and put it to bed," he says. Wysocki recalls receiving a letter from Buchanan's mother. "She said, 'Finally, no one looks at my son like he's a killer. That is forever gone.'" She thanked Wysocki for helping to uncover the truth. Wysocki says it remains the nicest letter she's ever received. It also serves as a reminder of what she calls the biggest lesson she's ever learned: "You don't just go by what someone says. You've gotta back it up."

Once the trial ended in June 2010, Wysocki decided she would retire her license. The case she cared about was closed. She didn't need to be camping out in her car tracking cheating spouses. That wasn't the life she sought. So per state requirements, she would write a letter to the Private Investigation and Polygraph Commission of the Tennessee Department of Commerce and Insurance, pay a small processing fee, and send back her licensing certificate and PI identification card. She had done what she'd set out to do. Angie's killer had been brought to justice and Wysocki didn't really have investigative ambitions beyond that.

This was a single-case calling.

"I was going back to being a mom and running the spa," Wysocki says. The slow burn of investigating would give way to simpler, more frequently gratifying occupational tasks. She'd be neither PI nor PITA.

She'd resume sleeping at night.

Instead, a television reporter named Dennis Ferrier ran a story about Wysocki on the local news in 2012. Ferrier had met Wysocki after she'd sent him a tip about a suspected sex offender working in a Nashville-area private school, but once he began learning about Wysocki's own back story, he wanted to cover her, too. Ferrier's story positioned Wysocki as an unflappable crime solver with preternatural investigative skills, a rare glimmer of hope for the hopeless whose loved ones died surrounded by questions—and whose questions have only grown louder over time. Wysocki hadn't formally retired her license, and was mainly working on rounding up auction items for a fund-raiser at her children's school.

That's when the letters and binders started pouring in. Wysocki was especially moved by those from parents who believed their children had been murdered and who had been left unsatisfied by the conclusions, or lack thereof, presented by the police.

Some of the mothers—"It always starts with the mothers," Wysocki says—had began doing investigative work of their own, assembling dossiers with page counts in the hundreds, laying out the details of their child's life, and, ultimately, of their untimely death. These mothers had done interviews, made timelines, and proposed theories—all of which started to pile up on Wysocki's desk.

The binders always included a range of tender photographs showing a now-deceased child at various ages: dressed excitedly for Halloween as a toddler, blowing out birthday candles as a grade-schooler, hugging a grandparent as a preteen, going to prom. It was as if communicating the fullness of their lives was a necessary step toward understanding their deaths. One mother, grieving for her teenaged son, drove to Wysocki's house with her binder and did so not having enough gas, or enough gas money, to get back home. Wysocki, a mother herself, understood that kind of urgency and couldn't turn her away. "All my focus had been on Angie or my kids up until then," Wysocki says. "And suddenly I had all this space. It was like, what do you do when your brain is freed?"

The outpouring of correspondence and the cries for help caused Wysocki not to retire her license and, also, to recalibrate her motivation. There were so many people seeking the kind of justice she had sought for Angie and now she had the skills to help them.

Though she couldn't know about the complications and traumas to come, those inherent in her line of work, she now understood that the vision of Angie wasn't merely calling her toward that single case—it was calling her toward a career.

"I didn't choose this," Wysocki says. "But I couldn't stop. I was just getting started."

2

As opposed to Wysocki, who intuited her way into being a PI in her forties, Mark Gillespie marked the profession as a goal when he was a boy. With an inherent knack for long-term strategic planning, the kind that behooves casework that can seem interminable, Gillespie, now sixty-one, and living in Austin, Texas, modeled his career path early on by jotting his aspirations on a series of three-by five-inch cards.

Gillespie has piercing blue eyes, a closely cropped salt-and-pepper goatee, and a crisply stylish haircut like one of the test pilots in *The Right Stuff*. As ex-military, a desire to dress in uniform, albeit a more casual one, persists. "Nice blue jeans, or Wranglers, a button-down point Oxford, or a short-sleeved Polo," he says. Gillespie makes it clear that despite being Texan, he does not wear a cowboy hat. "In this job, people need a clear view of your eyes," he says. He carries a Glock in a paddle holster, drives a pickup truck, and signs off on emails with a call to action: "Let's Roll."

Growing up as an Air Force brat, on bases from Japan to Virginia, Gillespie aimed, among other things, to become an Air Force officer like his dad. As a fan of *The Six Million Dollar Man*, a 1970s-era television series about a bionic military spy, Gillespie also decided he'd join the Office of Special Investigations, the global investigative branch of the Air Force, like the show's protagonist, Colonel Steve Austin.

Gillespie worked in the OSI as a classified federal agent for two decades, starting in 1979, with cases all around the world, ranging from drug trafficking to homicide to child molestation. While serving in the military, he also earned a master's degree in forensic science from George Washington University in 1983. Gillespie took an early retirement from the Air Force in 1996 and a few more goals remained: running a crime lab, which he did for the Austin Police Department, and teaching forensics at the college level; Gillespie helped develop the forensic science degree program at St. Edward's University in Austin. "That happened to be one of the fastest-growing degree programs at St. Ed's," he says.

In 2004, Gillespie hit one more career milestone by

starting a private investigation agency. "When I started," he says, "I advertised that I could do every kind of investigation because that's how I was trained." Having always worked in an institutional capacity, he was curious to explore a more entrepreneurial path. But Gillespie quickly realized PI work was a very different kind of job than the ones he had already known and excelled at. He had managed large investigative units in the military, planning and executing operations with teams numbering as many as forty people. As a member of the Austin PD, he had colleagues depending on him for DNA analysis (he started their DNA program) and at St. Edward's, he had his students.

As a new PI, however, Gillespie found himself increasingly alone. "I have a high need for inclusion," he says, "to be part of something." But Gillespie also felt liberated by his new status. Cases would no longer be assigned to him by a higher-up; he could seek out the kinds of cases he wanted to work and determine where his services were most needed.

More than a decade into being a PI, Gillespie is currently licensed in Texas, where he lives—and in two other Southern states. The Department of Public Safety regulates licensing for Texas PIs. A company owner like Gillespie holds the actual license, giving him the right both to conduct investigations and to hire others to do the same (eighteen and over, with no felony convictions, no place on any sex offender registry, no dishonorable discharge from the military). People who work for the owner of a PI company are called registrants.

As in Tennessee, there are barriers to entry. New recruits also cannot have been found mentally ill or unfit by a court. Registrants must not have been convicted for a misdemeanor in the previous half decade. And they must not have any current criminal charges leveled against them. Tennessee merely asks for "good moral character" and no substance abuse issues. Texas gets more technical about what makes one's character moral by requiring a fairly clean slate of convictions; however, they abstain from prying when it comes to drugs and booze.

Gillespie, who enjoys extra hoppy IPAs and whiskey, neat, in a Norlan Whiskey Glass, never worked as a registrant since his years of investigative experience with the Air Force's OSI opened the doors to the role of a licensee almost immediately. To gain a license in the state of Texas requires some form of pedigree, whether it's experiential (three years as a PI or 200 hours of training), academic (college graduate), or some combination of both (associates degree in criminal justice plus a year's investigative experience). Gillespie possessed a master's degree, ran an investigative lab for a large, metropolitan police department, and worked tens of thousands of hours cracking cases from the U.S.-Mexico border to South Korea. Still, ever humble, when Gillespie was applying for his Texas license, he sent letters to a number of local private investigators asking if they wanted to take him on as a registrant, just so he could gain a feel for the beat.

Most of them told Gillespie that they should be applying to work for him.

Shortly after filing his license application, Gillespie got word he'd met the qualifications and could proceed on to take the Private Security Manager's exam. Test takers have to answer 100 questions in two hours and though the exam is open book, one guide states that trying to the use the book as a crutch is a costly mistake. "It's nearly impossible to look up anything quickly in the Occupation Code and the Administrative Rules," says the study guide, which, itself, is 897 pages long.

Although Gillespie takes umbrage with the substance of the test—griping that it focuses too much on running a business and not enough on laws and investigative techniques—and says exams make him exceedingly anxious, he still passed easily on his first try.

A score of 70 percent is required; he notched a 99 percent, missing only one question.

FOR GILLESPIE, THE CALLS from disgruntled spouses came first. Infidelity, or the suspicion thereof, is the enduring gravy train of the PI industry. Busting cheaters can be a way of life. There's an endless supply of them. But those are hardly the cases that compel Gillespie, despite their ease (trail suspect, take photos), their volume, and their rate, which, he says, averages around $85 per hour. Instead, Gillespie is drawn toward investigations that pay less but have, what he feels, a far higher moral return.

Seventy-five percent of Gillespie's work involves indigent defense cases where a court-appointed criminal defense attorney and their accused client will hire Gillespie at just over $40 per hour to uncover enough facts to lessen a prison sentence or get a client off entirely.

"Most of them are murder charges," Gillespie says. "I'm not in this to make money. My passion is to help people in this type of situation, people with extremely limited resources, who are charged as a result of a flawed police investigation."

In the summer of 2007, Gillespie was called to the Travis

County Criminal Justice Center in Austin to meet with a nineteen-year-old Golden Gloves middleweight boxer named Kurtiss (pronounced Kur-teese) Evanjelous Ni'Quiez "Lucky" Colvin. Held on $215,000 bond, Colvin had been charged with manslaughter and misdemeanor assault after a forty-year-old housepainter named David Morales was beaten to death in the Booker T. Washington Terraces housing development, near where Colvin lived. Gillespie got to know Colvin, who maintained that he didn't kill anyone, in the jail's tiny visitation room. "It's dirty, maybe seven feet by ten feet. We're knee to knee," Gillespie says. "It's dark, dingy, and cold."

Even before taking on an investigation, Gillespie tries to develop a sense of who the client is and what he or she has, or has not, done. "First off," Gillespie says, "it's important that I believed Kurtiss." Gillespie, however, doesn't operate on faith alone. There were markers for truth, patterns he understood from years working in the OSI. "Kurtiss's passion for telling me his story was important," Gillespie says. Nonchalance may have indicated guilt. "He was consistent, he had emotion." In fact, Colvin cried.

Once Gillespie establishes a profile of his client, the hustle begins to attempt to corroborate it. Face-to-face interviewing is the way—and in this instance, that meant

Gillespie would be spending considerable amounts of time visiting the Booker T. Washington Terraces, a subsidized housing project in Austin. As a white, middle-aged, and middle-class former fed, Gillespie knew he might not be welcome there. The relationship between the community and law enforcement, which is how he'd be perceived even as a civilian investigator, was tenuous at best. "You're labeled a snitch if you're seen talking to people like that," Colvin says. "People don't talk. That's why it was so hard to get witnesses in my case."

Nevertheless, Gillespie rolled up to Colvin's neighborhood four days a week, almost every week for eighteen months. He'd park his pickup truck in front of one the low-slung red-brick buildings and begin talking to anyone in sight. When nobody was around, Gillespie would knock on doors, asking questions in an even, level tone.

"Just win their trust," he says. "Don't have an attitude. Don't play it like you're smarter or better. And let people know, 'I am *not* here to investigate you. I'm *not* a threat. I don't care what you're doing or if you're doing anything. I just need your help because some guy just like you, from where you're from, needs my help—and needs yours, too.'"

If Gillespie had one thing working in his favor, besides his own tact, it was the fact that the community felt immensely invested in Kurtiss Colvin and his prospects for a bright future. He'd been a high school track star and his prowess as a boxer seemed limitless: he might reach the Olympics or even attain a lucrative professional career. People in his neighborhood rooted for him; his success mattered to them. That being the case, it didn't take long for Gillespie to become known around the Booker T. Washington houses—and even around the Travis County Criminal Justice Center— as "Kurtiss's PI." Other potential clients started requesting Gillespie by lore alone: they wanted the man known as "Kurtiss's PI," to defend them, too.

By the end of the investigation, Gillespie had racked up nearly eighty interviews in service of reconstructing the events of the evening when the alleged incident occurred between Colvin and Morales. "Mark's a perfectionist," says Colvin. "He covers everything." According to Gillespie, Colvin was arrested after a car, driven by a thirty-six-year-old Hispanic male named Victor Medel, hit a two-year-old child on Thompson Street in the southwest corner of the Booker T. Washington Terraces. The *Houston Chronicle* reported that the toddler was "bumped." The *Austin Chronicle* reported, via an Austin Police Department press release, th the boy, Michael Hosea Jr., was "accidentally struck by a Ford Taurus" and that his injuries were "non-life threatening."

David Morales was the passenger in Medel's car.

He had reportedly gotten out of the vehicle to defend Medel as people surrounded the Taurus. One member of the growing mob, according to his arrest warrant, was Kurtiss Colvin. Morales ended up on the ground. Later, at a local hospital, he was declared dead from blunt force trauma to the head. Witnesses told police that Colvin had delivered the fatal blow. But, through months of dogged interviewing, Gillespie says he was able get many people to better recall what actually happened that night. Using prompts like drawn diagrams of the crowd and photographs of the street where the confrontation happened, he'd take them back through the night in question.

Gillespie operates from the standpoint that human memory is extremely fallible and, without question, aided by visual reminders. "If people don't see things on paper," he says, "they'll just make stuff up—because they really believe it or just to get rid of me." By making micro presentations to dozens of witnesses, Gillespie wasn't only able to put together a theory of what may have happened, he was able to figure out who threw the life-ending punch, the one the

Austin-American Statesman said caused the victim's "head to crack against the parking lot."

"We ended up finding the kid who actually did the damage," Gillespie says. He was sixteen. Colvin ultimately beat the manslaughter charges, though he was found guilty of aggravated assault. He'd made contact with Morales, he'd said, after he believed Morales was drawing a gun on him (no gun was found at the crime scene, though a box cutter was reportedly found in Morales's pocket). Colvin was sentenced by a jury to ten years' probation.

"He owes his life to me is what he says," Gillespie confesses. Letters Colvin wrote to Gillespie while incarcerated indicate that he believed his private investigator was a form of divine intervention and expressed utter surprise that anybody would go to such great lengths to help him.

Colvin's own father had been a disappointment and Gillespie, through his consistent presence and through his actions, had come to earn a kind of paternal role. "You've been nothing but a father figure to me," Colvin wrote.

ONE RECENT EVENING, SETTING his Let's Roll credo into motion, Gillespie took his friend John, who was interested in becoming a PI on a ride-along. Despite putting his university teaching days behind him, Gillespie still feels a responsibility to instruct and on top of welcoming curious parties to tag along on investigative work, he also gives lessons on firearms use and safety and teaches self-defense.

John and Gillespie made two stops. The first was to serve a cease and desist order. Gillespie had been hired by a man who'd become concerned with his daughter's safety. She'd been having an affair with a coworker, a military veteran suffering from post-traumatic stress disorder; he habitually beat her so badly that she had to seek treatment in an emergency room.

Gillespie drafted the cease and desist and a lawyer, paid by the client, put it on his letterhead to make it official. The letter cited "kicking, hitting, slapping, pushing and choking." It informed the recipient that, "choking a person with whom you've had a dating relationship is a third-degree felony in Texas with a punishment of up to ten years in prison."

The lawyer's signature was preceded by words written by Gillespie: "This is your final warning."

John wasn't merely there to survey the situation and decide whether he, too, would ever want to become a PI. He was there as extra muscle in case the man being served became violent. This is not unusual; Wysocki also brings backup when she thinks she may be in harm's way. On one recent job, she even brought along J. D. Skinner. "I needed a big body with a gun," she says. "Nobody's better than JD."

About serving the cease and desist, Gillespie said: "We were walking into an unknown and potentially dangerous situation. It would have been crazy to go in alone."

After a delivery without incident, Gillespie and his ride-along headed into another unpredictable environment, looking for two people living under a bridge in North Austin. The transients Gillespie was searching for had witnessed an incident he'd been investigating between two other homeless people: an alleged assault that he had reason to believe never happened. Gillespie's client was court appointed and had already spent nine months in jail awaiting trial. The people Gillespie was looking for, he figured, could prove no assault had taken place. "Finding them," he said, "was crucial to proving the allegations false."

Tracking people without addresses, phone numbers, or regular access to electricity, or mobile devices, Gillespie says, draws on consistent networking with a world that's totally off the grid. He's spent years learning who knows who and who lives where on the streets around Austin. Talking long-term with the city's homeless population is what enabled him and John to find his witnesses beneath an overpass on Interstate 35.

Before arriving at the bridge, Gillespie stopped at a gas station to buy beers for the people he intended to take statements from. "Beers and burgers go a long way," he told me. Cold drinks in hand, Gillespie approached the pair. "The environment reeked of alcohol, urine, and bird feces," he says, "and it takes patience and time for the conversation to open up, to gain their trust." Ultimately, Gillespie got the witness statements he needed. "Nobody attacked anybody else," he said. Afterward, his ride-along remarked on the surprising softness of his inquisition. Gillespie told his friend that was exactly his intention.

SOME OF GILLESPIE'S CASES can seem like mythological quests, sprawling epics that challenge his endurance and his resolve to find the truth. Just a few years after becoming a PI, he took on one such case in a town in the rural South; the investigation, life-threatening at times, would constantly feel to him like a steep and heavy uphill climb.

The name of the town, its exact location, and the names

of the parties involved must be obscured here to prevent identification. Despite Gillespie's investigative work, no formal case has been brought about by law enforcement against any person implicated in Gillespie's investigation. Everything here serves only to show how a private investigator does his job and does not assume or imply guilt of any person for any of the crimes investigated.

Whether or not a crime even happened is a central question of PI work and has yet to be legally established in this example. Gillespie's work on this case calls that question into relief at every turn.

It began with a June 2008 phone call from a colleague, a female Texas-based PI, who had been asked to look into the December 2007 death of an elderly widow (she'll be referred to throughout only as EW, for "elderly widow"). The family of the deceased had suggested that the small town in which they lived, though of little significance on the map was, in fact, rife with illegal activity, especially in regard to the drug trade, and that their elderly relative had been killed after threatening to expose its local kingpins to law enforcement.

The conditions surrounding the woman's death, quickly ruled a suicide before an autopsy could be performed, scared the female PI, who specializes mainly in child custody and missing persons cases, so she called Gillespie and asked if he would take the case instead.

He found himself drawn to it immediately.

A year later, Gillespie had become consumed by the case and the area in which it happened. His investigation had broadened beyond that first death to look into domestic abuse, child molestation, water theft, racketeering, fraud, police corruption, and narcotics trafficking. He opened nearly a dozen investigations in total. The town was broken, Gillespie thought. He wanted to do more than solve a case: he wanted to save a place that had gone rotten.

By the time Gillespie started posting signs around the town, more than a year into his work there, he had become a polarizing figure. Members of EW's family, who weren't paying him much to begin with, stopped paying him at all while still relying on his doggedness to solve what they regarded as a murder. Others around town, namely the ones Gillespie was investigating, simply wanted the PI gone. Gillespie, for his own part, grew even more determined to make his presence known. Ginning up public interest in his work might help him land witnesses and important testimony about the multitudes of possible crimes he was now looking into.

Not unlike the protagonist of the 2017 Oscar-winning film, *Three Billboards Outside Ebbing, Missouri*, who uses signage to express rage and to seek justice for the murder of her daughter, Gillespie put up a series of signs of his own. His, a decade prior to the film's release, were smaller, two feet by three feet, and professionally printed.

("I've never heard of that movie," Gillespie told me.)

One sign, in all-cap, red letters, read:

EW DID NOT COMMIT SUICIDE—SHE WAS MURDERED.
. . . AND THE MURDERERS ARE AMONG US.
YOU WILL SOON KNOW THE DETAILS AND
"IT WILL SHOCK YOU."
BUT, ON THE OTHER HAND, MAYBE IT WON'T!

Another of Gillespie's signs, black lettering on a taxi-yellow background, read:

BEWARE OF FALSE PROPHETS,
WHICH COME TO YOU IN SHEEP'S CLOTHING,
BUT INWARDLY THEY ARE RAVENING WOLVES.
(MATTHEW, 7:15—KJV)

The signs went up by the dozen. Gillespie posted them in the ground as if campaigning.

BEFORE EVEN GETTING TO town, Gillespie had been warned he wouldn't be entirely embraced there, or in the surrounding area. It was insular, he'd heard, and power was concentrated in a few select individuals—and that's precisely whom Gillespie would be investigating for obstructing justice and sweeping a possible murder under the rug. If he could collect enough evidence to prove murder, he'd also likely be cracking a drug ring of a size unknown to him.

Was it a local or regional business? Did it link to foreign cartels? Was it a national security issue?

When Gillespie first arrived, he booked a room in a motel until one of EW's nieces, who had been among her closest confidants, insisted Gillespie stay with her and her family. On many of his trips to the town, he took her up on her offer, staying in a guest room. On other trips, he'd stay in his RV, which he'd park on their land.

"I became like an adopted brother," Gillespie says. "They'd cook like you wouldn't believe. Everything from scratch. It wasn't grab-a-frozen-sausage-biscuit and heat it up. It was grits, the slow kind. I basically camped out with them, on and off, for the next four years." He even started calling EW what they had called her, putting the word "Aunt" before an endearing diminutive of her real name.

Since there's no reciprocity between Texas's private investigator license and that of the new state Gillespie would be working in, he began fresh. The new state's application form was different. It asked if an applicant had been court-martialed or if he or she had "supported any movement, group or organization which advocates the overthrow of the government of the United States of America." It asked for three letters of recommendation and required answers to fifteen written questions about one's actual experiences as a PI.

Once officially licensed, Gillespie began his investigation in earnest. He spoke to EW's daughters and started piecing together a profile of their mother's life. Local police said EW died a from a self-inflicted gunshot wound, but her daughters told Gillespie that they didn't believe that could be the case.

They told Gillespie their mother was lively and acted much younger than her eighty-five years. She was considered a "health nut" by her family and frequently went out dancing and to the casinos. EW was described as "strong and tough" and as a survivor. "She suffered her entire marriage," one daughter told Gillespie. "Dad made her suffer." The same daughter went on to describe her father's actions toward her mother as physical, emotional, and sexual abuse. "He tore her up inside so bad that she required surgery," she said. "After he died she started to enjoy herself."

The other daughter told Gillespie that local law enforcement had covered up her mother's death and that a prominent religious official was in on it, too. Gillespie eventually came to liken the man's grip on the town to that of a cult leader—the man swayed legal issues by manipulating his congregants to stay silent and not report things they felt were crimes.

That daughter also had her suspicions about the tenant who farmed her mother's land, a rising local business leader who flew planes, owned a trucking company, and would go on to run the local airport authority and the levee district. "Here's a guy who controlled every way and in and out of town," Gillespie says. In his case reports, Gillespie would ultimately refer to these two men, whom he considered to be suspects, as "the Preacher" and "the Rancher."

In attempting to speak to everybody who had seen EW

in the days prior to her death, Gillespie learned that she was a creature of habit. Her routines mattered to her; her house-keeping was constant and precise. One confidential informant who asked Gillespie to withhold her name from any reports for fear of retaliation, told him that she had visited EW the day before her death and noted EW had already set up her coffee for the next morning, as if she'd fully expected to brew it.

Another friend remembered speaking to EW on Wednesday evening, just hours before her death, about the book he was reading by the Reverend Billy Graham. "She asked if she could read it when I was finished," the friend said. One of EW's daughters told Gillespie that her mother had asked a close friend if she wanted to go to a nearby casino that same night. "Does that sound like anyone that was going to kill themselves?" the daughter said.

Family members and EW's doctor all told Gillespie that she had no history of depression, despite the coroner listing it, along with a "gun shot wound (GSW) to chest (cardiac area)" as her cause of death. (Listing "depression" as an actual cause of death is, in Gillespie's view, inexplicable.) In an affidavit, one of EW's daughter's makes her belief clear: "We know she didn't commit suicide," she said. "This is murder."

What was believed, by certain relatives, friends, and neighbors Gillespie interviewed, was that EW knew a secret. "About two weeks before [my aunt] died she was very upset and she told me she was going to expose some stuff," said a niece. "She was tired of them using her house as a whorehouse when she was gone and she was fixing to expose a lot of stuff."

The man said to be using the house for sexual escapades, per affidavits, was the Rancher.

Because he farmed the land surrounding EW's house, the Rancher had a key to it, which EW had given to him. Allegedly, the Rancher, though a married father of three, carried on extramarital affairs with multiple women. EW also believed that the Rancher was having sex with different women in her bed—and in his combine out in the fields. To complicate matters further, several family members told Gillespie that EW, eighty-five, was both in love with and having a sexual relationship with the Rancher despite him being four decades younger.

Interviewing one of EW's nieces, Gillespie learned that she had recently seen a low-flying plane out near her aunt's property. "It was flying straight towards us," she said. "It swooped really low and then picked back up." The niece immediately called her Aunt.

"Yup, they are dropping drugs," EW told her, nonchalantly. "She said it so calmly," the niece informed Gillespie, "as though she knew all about it and she wasn't surprised."

Gillespie learned that the week before EW died, she had attended a family gathering where she seemed agitated and told relatives, "I'm tired of all this shit; it is coming down. I'm going to expose it, y'all. And y'all are going to be shocked."

(Eventually, her language was echoed by Gillespie on his posted signs.)

Another event from EW's social calendar was also highlighted for Gillespie. A couple months before her death, EW attended a dinner with the Rancher. He called the gathering a "pilot's club meeting" and it was said to be attended by some of the people in town who owned and/or flew small planes. The Preacher was there along with a handful of others. Gillespie had heard that the dinner had upset EW. He'd also heard that she had seen a stash of illegal drugs at a local airstrip. When Gillespie tried to access its hangar himself, he found the property to be heavily protected and impossible to enter.

One of EW's children told Gillespie that suddenly her mother had a whole vocabulary she didn't previously possess, dropping references to milligrams and scales into her conversations. Another source told Gillespie that EW was killed because she'd come to know too much. "I believe that's why they got rid of her," said the source. "I believe what she saw got her killed. It was drugs that got her killed and she wouldn't tell us. If she had told us we could have helped her."

Not everybody bought into this idea, Gillespie discovered. A nephew of EW's told him that suicide is simply hard to accept and it's not surprising that other family members would substitute acceptance with storytelling.

Still, as Gillespie kept talking his way around town, he found out that EW had been spending nights at other relatives' homes more frequently.

Her own home had recently been broken into, and she had said to a daughter that she wanted to close up her house, which was out on the lonely outskirts of town, and move to a place where she'd be closer to people. It was too quiet where she lived. Anybody could get away with anything, she felt. Somebody, she'd said, had been standing outside her home at night, smoking cigarettes, bent on intimidating her. EW was also spooked by her neighbor, an elderly man who, Gillespie learned, also felt vulnerable in his surroundings, patrolling his land throughout the night with guns strapped to his chest.

Years of Gillespie's forensics training triggered a series of questions about EW's death. He had in his possession a series of photographs of her corpse, not ones taken and shared by the local police or coroner, but, rather, shots her daughter had snapped in haste at the morgue after being told she couldn't view her mother's body. The photos, Gillespie says, show an unusual bloodstain pattern on her hands, a number of bruises inconsistent with a self-inflicted gunshot wound, and broken fingers that would suggest a struggle with a perpetrator. Further, that daughter told Gillespie she'd spotted a series of knotty bruises on her mother's head (he says they're consistent with being struck repeatedly) and grip bruises, those formed by her being grabbed hard, are evident on EW's wrists.

Although Gillespie filed a Freedom of Information request to obtain any police or medical examiner's files on EW's death, he received no cooperation from the sheriff or the coroner and found it perplexing that law enforcement wouldn't share details of a case they merely believed to be a suicide.

The more Gillespie heard about the crime scene, the

more he believed a cover-up was in play. He had learned that a relative of EW's had been instructed by a deputy to clean up a pool of her blood with bleach—and he did. Additional blood spatter was found as far away as the kitchen and in the garage, on the car. (Gillespie tested the scene with luminol, presumptively confirming the spread-out presence of blood.) Had EW been fighting back against somebody, Gillespie wondered?

If she shot herself in her chair, where the bullet hole had been found, did she then get up to walk around the house, trailing blood everywhere before returning to her seat to die? She kept her own gun in her car. Was the blood spatter near the vehicle evidence of EW trying to reach her firearm so she could somehow defend herself?

Further, the chair in which EW was found was taken outside her home and incinerated not long after her body was discovered. It went up in flames in her yard. The most important piece of evidence, perhaps, had been destroyed. The throw rugs, which usually bordered the chair, also went missing in a home where everything had its precise place. Gillespie says three guns were found scattered on the floor: a .410, a .25, and a .38. Did an eighty-five-year-old woman need three firearms to kill herself? Strangely, EW's door was unchained, an anomaly for a woman who chained her door nightly and had lately felt even more of a need to attend to her locks. Had she let her killer in herself? She'd only have opened her door for somebody she knew. All of her relatives told Gillespie as much.

The questions only snowballed. Gillespie found it suspicious that the person who found EW's body was, of all people, the Rancher—the same man she was purportedly ready to out for narcotics possession. The Rancher had then called the Preacher, whose planes were thought to also move drugs. It's unknown who first called the police or if there's even a 911 recording and, says Gillespie, it's possible the Rancher or the Preacher just dialed a local law enforcement officer who was simply on their side.

That the Rancher first called the Preacher, the town's de facto high authority and his possible drug dealing associate, and not EW's family, raised a red flag for Gillespie, too. He wanted to know why EW's body was cremated before a full autopsy could be performed and wanted to find out whether, as he'd heard, the Rancher was at the crime scene deleting numbers from EW's phone.

———

THE MORE TIME GILLESPIE spent investigating EW's death, the more problems he learned about throughout the town and its adjacent areas. He describes the entire location as "out of sight, out of mind" and says its remoteness contributes to a feeling of lawlessness. "It's the perfect storm," he says "for undetected illegal activity."

Since Gillespie's background is in military intelligence, he conducted his work around town like an OSI operation, developing sources, snitches, and informants. There are no hacks in this type of PI work. You talk to people until they trust you or until you decide they never will. You go slow. You listen, then listen harder. You use your gut, but not independent of the facts. You don't get emotional as a reaction to others. You exemplify calm. You nod along. You dig in. You wait. You remember the questions that weren't answered to your liking. You reframe them at a later point in time and see whether the answers change. Having been trained to write comprehensive reports about his cases, Gillespie still depends on writing to clarify his case work and to leave a written record of his process.

His paper trail from these cases is more than 500 pages long.

"You were either in one camp or another," he says, of the

area's residents, "on the right side of the law, or the wrong side." One source Gillespie developed over a period of years took him out "to the middle of nowhere" to see evidence of local meth labs. "According to him, he used to work for the Mexican cartels. He knew a lot about the local drug activity," Gillespie says. "I didn't know if I could trust him at first. I was armed to the teeth at our first meeting. But I developed him until he became a trusted agent of mine."

Gillespie conducted interviews on porch steps, in the middle of fields, or deep in the woods, swarming with mosquitoes. One guy raised cock-fighting roosters, and the birds strutted all around as Gillespie interviewed his source, who didn't want to be seen with the PI, by candlelight in his henhouse. Other sources would tell Gillespie stories about local law enforcement cruising the nearby river in swamp boats and picking up bales of narcotics that had been dropped for them by traffickers in the river. "I spent countless nights looking for that kind of activity," Gillespie says. "I never saw it, but the stories went on and on. Everybody just accepted it because they were scared for their lives."

As Gillespie stayed on in the area, digging ever deeper into EW's case, other investigations arose and metastasized. EW's niece, with whom Gillespie was staying, and her twin sister, introduced him to a friend of theirs who said her husband had been beating her for years and that he molested her daughter, too (she'll be referred to only as NF, for "niece's friend"). Gillespie began looking into it. The husband had worked for the Preacher and every time she sought his counsel, and the strength, and perhaps the permission, to find a way out of her marriage, he'd dismiss her as high-maintenance and as an insubordinate spouse.

One of the factors that kept Gillespie in town so long was that people kept telling him terrible things; he couldn't walk away from them. While taking NF's affidavit, she told Gillespie that the Preacher could have put an end to the abuse, saving both her and her underage daughter from additional harm. "He could have come to bat for me and helped me," NF says. "Instead, he tore me down."

Understanding that he was dealing with a strain of small town omertà that suppressed the true functions of law enforcement and quashed public agency and outcry, Gillespie created two separate websites through which investigative tips could be submitted, either signed or anonymously, while he investigated other sexual abuse cases in the area.

One abuse case linked back to his original investigation:

it involved a great-nephew of EW. According to witnesses, the nephew had been seen near EW's home the morning her body was discovered. He was reportedly standing by the roadside, looking strung out and panicked. Later, says Gillespie, he was seen buying drinks for patrons at a local bar and bragging that he had suddenly just come into a large sum of money.

One of Gillespie's theories is that the nephew, a known substance abuser, spousal abuser, and alleged child molester, was paid by the Preacher and the Rancher to kill his great-aunt. Gillespie theorizes that she would have opened the door for him. He believes the nephew would have been capable of anything.

Another tip led Gillespie to investigate the town's then–chief of police, whom he was told arrested people at will by forcing them to admit guilt on a signed document and then releasing them from his custody after accepting a cash payoff. While looking into those allegations, conducting interviews, and producing affidavits to build a case, Gillespie also heard stories about the chief sexually harassing citizens and conducting a drug ring of his own.

Ultimately, the local church began speaking out against Gillespie, equating him with Satan. "Church officials were telling the congregation I was the devil," Gillespie says. "They were telling them not to talk to me, to stay away from me." Gillespie says the Preacher's followers would go around taking down his signs and he'd just put more right back up.

"There's always more signs," he says.

Threats came Gillespie's way from below the pulpit, too. When he tried interviewing the Rancher, he recalls being met with hostility. Gillespie spotted him on the road in his truck and followed him home. "I wanted to confront him," Gillespie says. As an investigator, he needed to. The confrontation consisted of a "Get the fuck out of here and don't ever come back. You better watch yourself," Gillespie recalls. Elsewhere, Gillespie remembers being sneered at. "People would come up and tell me to get out of town, not to come back," he says. One person he was investigating made repeated death threats and once attempted to run Gillespie's truck off the road at high speeds and into a body of water.

At the same time, Gillespie's personal life back in Austin was taking a hit. All the travel was hurting his marriage. Though Gillespie spoke with his wife, Cheryl, on a near-daily basis, he knew his absence made things tough for her. Financial strain set in, too. EW's case, and the subsequent others, paid a pittance, a fraction of even the indigent defense cases Gillespie would take back in Texas. As his income plummeted, his client also became increasingly dissatisfied with his efforts. "She wanted me to only spend time investigating her mom's death," Gillespie says.

Still, even with domestic and financial tensions mounting, Gillespie didn't want to stop what he started. He felt responsible for the well-being of the town. Private investigation, however, can only go so far without help from law enforcement. As much as private investigators can effectively act like another arm of the law, at a certain point they can also become like a phantom limb: the information they collect in the name of justice, no matter how compelling, is notional— a feeling, detached—until law enforcement agrees to give it a physical shape in the form of warrants, arrests, trials, verdicts, and sentencings. All a PI can do is find facts. They have no power to take further action on their own.

Gillespie couldn't manage to get any kind of help from law enforcement with EW's case. The tiny local police department, he surmised, were busy running their own racket. In December 2009, Gillespie wrote a two-page letter to the sheriff with a laundry list of investigative requests. Gillespie wanted the 911 tape alerting the sheriff of EW's death. He asked to see the sheriff's own investigation report along

with its supporting materials like photographs and video-
tapes. Transcripts of radio and mobile data terminal communication were summoned by Gillespie as were evidence
logs, crime scene entry control logs, and any request for forensic analysis.

Further, Gillespie wanted a rundown of all personnel
who responded to the crime scene. He wanted to study the
operating and training procedures for crime scene investigations and death investigations, including, per his memo,
"suicide, unattended deaths, homicide, accidental deaths,
other." Were the officers on the case even qualified to do
this kind of investigation? Gillespie wondered.

Gillespie also asked to review the personnel file of the
deputy who was first on the scene at EW's house and, ultimately and unwaveringly, concluded that she shot herself
dead. Gillespie sought to go over that deputy's disciplinary
actions, commendations, training records, and duty assign-
ments. The sheriff responded to Gillespie's letter by text
message, offering to speak to him. But the conversation, he
says, never happened. He didn't know why.

When Gillespie called the FBI about one of these investigations, the FBI acknowledged the phone call with a June
2010 letter saying they weren't interested in investigating it.

In November 2010, Gillespie tried yet another route, presenting his assorted cases to a task force comprised of federal agents and members of the state police. Gillespie felt optimistic about the opportunity, thinking his detailed presentation would compel at least one law enforcement body to act. Instead, a few weeks later he found out that the targets of his investigation had somehow acquired copies of his presentation. Fearing a leak, he says he subsequently lost trust in those agencies, too.

When Gillespie sent a letter to the district attorney in the fall of 2011, concerning yet another sexual abuse of a minor case he had been working, he received a response back months later, signed by the DA.

"Mark, our office does not have the resources to undertake investigations," it read. "For this and other reasons I can't take the actions requested by you." Nobody in law enforcement, it seemed, was prepared to give Gillespie an inch.

The attorney general's office responded to Gillespie with a letter telling him his 2011 complaint to them simply got lost.

As the rejection letters piled up, Gillespie felt it was time to take a step back. He had started EW's case only four years into becoming a PI, and though he failed to get the results he wanted, he sees the experience as formative.

"It helped me shape my professional direction," he says. "It made me realize firsthand just how corrupt our system can be, and how you've really got to fight for justice. Gillespie also makes it clear that he never formally resigned from the case.

"I never said, 'That's it,'" he says. "I'm actually thinking about reviving it all."

Deep into Nashville's Gaylord Opryland Resort & Convention Center—a sprawling glass-topped ecosystem with waterfalls, a couple dozen restaurants, its own indoor riverboat and thousands of guests illuminated by thousands more hanging twinkle lights—Sheila Wysocki has taken her seat on CrimeCon's Podcast Row.

CrimeCon, launched in 2017 at the JW Marriott in Indianapolis, brings together all facets of true crime entertainment and crime solving, from justice-seeking, televised ratings machines like Nancy Grace to authors of novels and memoirs to podcasters who host shows like *Martinis & Murder* and *Wine & Crime* with collective listenership climbing into the millions. Wysocki's booth is just across the way from the one with the producers of *Atlanta Monster* and *Up and Vanished*, a podcast that used journalism to ultimately help solve a murder.

The 2018 edition of CrimeCon is three times the size

of its predecessor, and *People* magazine listed the three-day gathering in early May, along with *60 Minutes* and the Grand Canyon, as one of their "Top Hundred Reasons to Love America." You can buy a CrimeCon T-shirt for $25 or a sweatshirt for $45. The CrimeCon corkscrew costs ten bucks.

Attendees, mostly women, fill cavernous conference rooms for discussions with ex-FBI agents or ex–Manson family members. They can hear a career prosecutor discuss what it's like to choose juries for death penalty cases. There are workshops on identifying serial perpetrators and liars. Attendees have traveled from all fifty states and six countries, paying as much as $1,000 per person for a platinum badge with line-skipping privileges and one-on-one sit-down meetings with the crime solver of their choice. Base-level tickets sell at the door for $179.

Amid the unavoidable commercialism of the enterprise, Wysocki is hoping to use her platform here to help find out what happened to the children of two families who have hired her to investigate their deaths.

The podcast that landed Wysocki on Podcast Row, like her investigation agency, is called *Without Warning* and will focus on the July 2015 death of Lauren Agee, a twenty-year-

old Ball State criminal justice student who was found floating, facedown, in Center Hill Lake, a man-made body of
water in central Tennessee. The lake branches into dozens
of hollows and creeks over its sprawl of nearly thirty square
miles. On a map, it looks like an unsightly and unmanage-
able outburst of varicose veins.

Agee had attended Wakefest there, a weekend-long wakeboarding festival, with a group of friends; she never made
it home. Her mother and stepfather, Sherry and Michael
Smith, hired Wysocki not long after local police closed the
case, having decided that Lauren died as the result of an
accidental fall off a cliff. Wysocki decided to launch a podcast to further her investigation, which has been ongoing
since early 2016. Maybe, she thought, if she went as public
as possible with her findings thus far, the rest of the evidence needed to go to trial, or uncover the truth, would
finally surface.

Crowdsourcing a case is an unconventional approach
among PIs. The chance of inundating the investigation
with false-information increases significantly. Sherry Smith
has, in fact, received what amounts to cruel pranks via Facebook, where anonymous sources have told her they know
who killed Lauren—and they have it on tape. But Wysocki

is willing to roll the dice in launching a more public campaign. She knows how to quickly identify and discard false tips and she believes the goodwill ultimately outweighs the bad.

In effect, she's deputizing a much larger crime-solving team than she ever could have before, not unlike what a hotel marketing executive named John Walsh did with *America's Most Wanted*, the 1988 television show he created to hunt down criminals after the murder of his six-year-old son Adam (Callahan Walsh, another of Walsh's sons, and a former producer for the show, which ran for twenty-five seasons, tracking down over a thousand wrongdoers, is speaking at CrimeCon as well).

Wysocki's other reason for being here, on CrimeCon's opening evening, is to lead a breakout session called The PI Experience, an equally unconventional investigative experiment.

Standing up from her seat on Podcast Row, Wysocki begins making her way through the crowd toward the Ryman Ballroom, one floor beneath the concourse of podcasters.

"We're having three hundred and seventy people tonight," Wysocki says. "There were supposed to be two hundred."

The plan is to divide the crowd into fourteen groups, each of which will be guided by a PI through the different elements of the 2014 death of a young man named Jonathan Crews.

WHEN PAM CREWS, JONATHAN'S mother, got hold of Wysocki in October 2014, at the behest of her lawyer, Tom Shaw, Wysocki was ready to retire her PI license for a second time. This time, she feared continuing on in the role.

Work Wysocki had done on another homicide case, looking into the death of a twenty-year-old nursing student named Holly Bobo, had drawn the ire of the Tennessee Bureau of Investigation. Wysocki had developed a theory about the case, one that conflicted with the TBI's. "I showed their investigation to be junk," she says.

Wysocki believes the TBI wanted to undermine her reputation. In 2013, the TBI released a statement suggesting she was running a scam. They publically called her a liar and they showed up at her house, she says, to intimidate and interrogate her and seize computer files. They also subpoenaed Google, she says, to access any information she had on their servers, such as emails, images, or Google Docs. She says they harassed her for more than a year, through mid-2014. Wysocki ultimately felt so threatened and tortured by the TBI, that she decided to relocate to another state and quit PI work altogether. "That's when I realized the 'good guys' weren't always the 'good guys,'" she says.

(Verdicts from the Bobo case, handed down in 2017 and 2018 confirmed Wysocki's investigations as correct; a TBI agent admitted during one of the trials that they had made significant mistakes during their investigation, missing critical clues and focusing on the wrong leads. Wysocki says she's still waiting for an apology.)

After her ordeal with the TBI, Wysocki was planning, again, to retire as a PI. The TBI, she figured, could make her life, and her family's life, a living hell. She had publically embarrassed them and they were, after all, the law. What choice did she have, she thought, but to live a more low-key life and to let the authorities rule, whether justly or not?

"Pam's voice changed everything," Wysocki says. Yet another police investigation had gone awry. Yet another family had no answers and sorely needed them. Jonathan Crews had been about the same age as Wysocki's oldest son. "I heard Pam's voice and knew I had to fight harder than ever before," Wysocki says. "That could have been my kid."

Jonathan Crews's girlfriend at the time, Brenda Lazaro, has not been arrested or charged in his death, but circumstances and evidence challenge the conclusion that Crews died when he allegedly shot himself in the heart, either as a suicide or an accident, during an argument with Lazaro.

JONATHAN CREWS DIED IN his own bed, in unit 813 of the Riverchase Apartments, in Coppell, Texas, a suburb of Dallas, on February 2, 2014. He was proud of having just recently moved in. At twenty-seven, it was the first time he could afford to live alone. Jonathan, who was six feet three, with blue eyes and sandy-brown hair, had graduated from Baylor University with a degree in history and had been managing an urgent care and occupational therapy center in the year before his death. He had a corgi, Ulysses, named for the hero of the epic ancient Greek poem, *The Odyssey*.

After Jonathan died, his parents, Pam, an artist, and John, an attorney and then the pastor of the Heartland Church, received condolences from his coworkers. They described Jonathan's personality as magnetic, his spirit, indelible. The wife of another coworker left a comment on Pastor Crews's blog, remembering the time his son threw her a baby shower. "His heart was enormous," she wrote, "bigger than this world." Crews was even fondly remembered by the cashier where he frequently bought donuts and kolaches for his coworkers. When Pam Crews informed the staffer at the donut shop that Jonathan had passed away, "She remembered," Pam wrote in an email to Coppell Police Department detectives, "exactly what he used to buy and boxed it all up for us, without charge."

About six months before his death, in November of 2013, Jonathan Crews began dating Brenda Lazaro. His sister, Dani, introduced them after she befriended Lazaro at the Wu Yi Shaolin Martial Arts Center, where Dani took classes along with Pam and Jonathan. Lazaro worked there as an assistant instructor. According to Wu Yi's website, the style of kung fu taught at the school, My Jhong Law Horn, is based on "deception and mobility." According to a grand master of the form, the fighting style, on top of instilling discipline in its students, is meant to "leave a defendant confused and vulnerable to My Jhong Law Horn's deadly blows." Lazaro's instructor photo on the site shows her crouching and extending a silver sword. Her dark hair is pulled back off her face. Her gaze is unbreakable; her arms, sinewy.

Before asking Lazaro out, Crews, ever chivalrous, asked his sister for permission, not wanting to intrude on their friendship. He also asked permission from Henry Su, who ran the martial arts studio and seemed to be a father figure to Lazaro. A few months after he and Lazaro started dating, Crews introduced her to two close friends, Emily Tadie and Jacob Ramsey, who were then dating and are now married. Tadie and Ramsey's approval was critical to Crews. Every time he had a new girlfriend, according to his mother, they'd have to "pass the Emily and Jacob test." When the two couples all met at a Chinese restaurant, Lazaro remained mostly silent throughout the meal, stewing over the fact that Tadie had hugged Crews hello.

Lazaro exhibited acute jealousy throughout her relationship with Crews. She questioned him obsessively when other women liked his Facebook posts. She requested that Crews block his ex-girlfriend, Humma Tajuddin, from following him. Lazaro had even messaged Tajuddin, pretending to be Crews; Pam Crews recalls that message being unnecessarily nasty. And Lazaro just couldn't let go of that initial hug between her boyfriend and his good friend Tadie.

While Crews visited Germany over Christmas that year, he and Lazaro texted back and forth, with her interrogating him over even his most casual interactions with other women while he responded back, trying to gain her trust.

On Christmas morning, they nearly broke up. Lazaro confessed to Crews how hard it would be for her if he ended it. "I just feel I was right after all and that you are going to end by leaving me," she wrote (having split her childhood between Mexico and the United States, Lazaro's English was imperfect). "Is just too much." But they didn't finalize the breakup. Instead, they smoothed things over.

It's questionable whether Crews knew all that much about Lazaro's extensive history with extreme jealousy, but even if he had it may not have been a deterrent since Pam Crews described her son's dating tendencies as "a pick-up-the-broken-baby-bird kind of thing." Pam Crews revealed in an email to Detective Maurer at the Coppell Police Department, that Lazaro told him that she had attempted suicide seven years before they got together and that she had scars on her arms and wrists. "He was still fact-finding to see if it was a viable long-term relationship," Pam Crews wrote.

Matthew Kirk, however, had dated Lazaro prior to Crews, for four years, beginning in 2009, and talked about her like she was poison. Tadie led Wysocki to Kirk, and as soon as Wysocki heard about Kirk's existence, she went right for him.

Wysocki prefers to motor from one interview to the next, working fourteen- to sixteen-hour days. A simple Google search revealed that Kirk worked with his mother at a Dallas-area insurance brokerage. Wysocki drove over and found him in a sparsely decorated office, carrying a coffeepot. *There's my guy*, she thought.

Wysocki told Kirk why she was there. He didn't want to talk. The mere mention of Lazaro's name made him look, Wysocki says, as if he had been punched. Wysocki followed him back to his desk. "I'm still asking you the questions whether you want to talk or not," Wysocki says, of her interviewing style. She was sure to tell Kirk the series of lies that Lazaro had told Crews about him: that he worked at Walmart, that he was broke and going nowhere. She told him he could be the hero of the case. Wysocki showed up at Kirk's office four times, in total, over the course of her investigation. "I never call first," she says. "Why would I call people? You want to catch them off guard. By the end, with Matthew Kirk, he was telling me everything."

In a later deposition, given under oath on April 28, 2016, with Wysocki present and Crews's family attorney, Tom Shaw, asking the questions, Kirk spends ninety-seven minutes offering what amounts to a damning composite of Lazaro's character. Wysocki's initial interview and re-cording of Kirk was critical to Shaw's line of questioning. Shaw says Wysocki's interrogation of Kirk will ultimately be critical to his case. "I'm going to play that deposition start to finish during the trial," he says.

In the deposition video, Kirk, with a shaved head, slate-colored blazer, and a gray dress shirt beneath, is, once again agitated that he's being asked to talk about Brenda Lazaro at all. He had just gotten married a few weeks before. "I'm try-ing to forget that girl," he says of Lazaro, raising his voice and intensifying his gesticulations, "She almost ruined my life . . . that girl ruined the relationship between me and my family . . . and almost ruined me."

Kirk says all he wanted to do was help Lazaro and that he worked really hard to do so. He urged her to seek therapy and she did. Still, the relationship was such a strain on Kirk, he says, that he sought mental health treatment for himself as well: "She drove me to a point where I had to go to a psychologist," he says. After almost a half decade together, Lazaro broke up with Kirk, he says, via text message. "She put me down pretty badly," he concludes.

In his deposition, Kirk tells Shaw that Lazaro had a traumatic upbringing: "A really rough background." When

Lazaro was younger, she had told Kirk she witnessed a murder, but she didn't tell him much more other than the fact that somebody was killed in the street in Mexico where she spent part of her childhood.

"If that girl doesn't want to talk about something," Kirk says in the deposition, "she won't talk about it. Good luck questioning her."

"She was jealous of every woman I talked to," Kirk continued, "She got crazy whenever I went around any girl." Lazaro issued constant ultimatums to Kirk—"It's me or her," she'd say—while simultaneously looking for constant reassurance, which Kirk provided. Lazaro's obsessive sense of envy even extended to Kirk's sister-in-law; Lazaro didn't like the way she hugged him just like she didn't like the way Tadie hugged Crews. When Kirk wanted to visit his sister-in-law in the hospital after she gave birth to his niece, Lazaro forbade it. Nevertheless, Kirk went, only to return home to find Lazaro sobbing and bleeding. She had intentionally cut herself.

According to Kirk, Lazaro often practiced self-harm. She was erratic, sometimes pulling her hair and banging her head against the wall. Kirk called the police twice, asking them to take Lazaro to a hospital where she could stabilize.

Whenever Kirk would ask for Lazaro to explain her behavior, he says, she'd simply start to cry.

On February 1, 2014, Crews texted his sister, Dani, confiding in her in regards to his own problematic relationship with Lazaro. They'd been fighting in ways that made Crews uncomfortable. By all accounts, he was a peacemaker, drama-free, a stabilizing force for those around him. And Crews was increasingly concerned that Lazaro would soon ask him to cast aside his friendship with Emily Tadie, and, effectively, with Jacob Ramsey, who had been Crews's college roommate and best friend since ninth grade.

Crews laid out four options for how to deal with Lazaro in his texts to his sister. He could 1) "Fight to try to make it better which will probably never happen." 2) "Choose Brenda." 3) "Refuse to give up either and see if Brenda ends it." Or 4) "End it with Brenda now."

Weighing those options himself, Crews surmised, via text, that the first three options "all hold a strong likelihood of ending the relationship," but that the fourth option is likely the kindest as "it limits/contains the damage." Later that day, Crews told his sister the breakup was forthcoming.

On the morning of February 2, Crews texted Ramsey asking if he wanted to grab some food. Before eating at a favorite Tex-Mex restaurant nearby, Ramsey and Tadie both came over to check out Crews's new apartment. Like Crews, Ramsey was a lifelong firearms enthusiast and he had a look at Crews's guns. Crews's Tavor rifle was new and his SIG Sauer pistol, stored meticulously, was loaded with a round in its chamber. Later that night, the SIG would end Crews's life. The magazine would be stashed elsewhere. And an unlikely sounding story would emerge that perhaps Crews didn't realize there was a single bullet in the chamber.

At lunch, Tadie and Ramsey noticed Crews was acting strangely. Later, they realized why: Crews was upset about how Lazaro would respond to it not just being a guys' lunch. Tadie was there. That hug, and the problems it caused, was still looming. Crews, not one to lie about his whereabouts, knew there'd be consequences and Lazaro, predictably, called Crews during the meal, asking whom he was with.

When she found out Tadie had joined them, she asked Crews to put her on the phone. Tadie recalls being yelled at and being called a "disrespectful little girl." Ramsey recalls, much to his surprise, the call made Tadie cry. Crews apologized for Lazaro's behavior and told his friends he was planning on ending the relationship with her imminently. They accompanied him back home to the Riverchase Apartments and finally left around 2:00 p.m.

That night, at 10:52 p.m., Tadie received a text from Crews's phone. "I want to die," it said. Nothing about that text's substance, its tone, or its brevity made any sense. Crews's written messages were typically long and generous, not morbid, cryptic, or worrisome. He was upbeat and helpful. Wanting to die, and conveying it out of nowhere, via text, seemed like so much of an anomaly that it must have been fiction.

Wysocki believes it was Lazaro who sent Tadie the message.

THE DOORS TO THE Ryman Ballroom are opened and the crowd rushes in. A woman named Becky Drumwright sits down next to me, a few rows back from the stage. Becky met Wysocki after she drove to her house to tell her the story of her son, Tony's death: she's the woman who didn't have enough gas, or gas money, to get back home after laying out her son's case in Wysocki's living room. Wysocki has been looking into the circumstances of Tony Drumwright's death ever since.

At 8:45 p.m., with all the PI Experience attendees seated, the recorded sound of a woman crying begins playing loudly over the speakers, following an automated time stamp of "23:30 and 39 seconds."

"Oh my God, oh my God," says the woman, choking on her words, trying to catch her breath. A 911 dispatcher attempts to settle the caller and determine her location. She yelps, "He's shooting himself in the heart, and he's dying right now."

The dispatcher asks the woman, "Did he do it on purpose?"

"No!" she says. But the woman quickly changes her answer, "Yeah!" she says. "He did it on purpose."

Much of the rest of the call is about the dispatchers working to get an address out of the caller despite her being able to identity where she is in a variety of ways. She knows, early in the call, she's in unit 813. She confirms cross streets, the apartment complex's name, and even that she's north of the McDonald's, despite continuously saying she doesn't know where she is. "Oh my God," she says. "Jonathan, Jonathan."

When the dispatchers ask her to go knock on a neighbor's door to confirm the address, she knocks in the manner of somebody going next door to borrow flour to make muffins, not somebody whose boyfriend is bleeding out. About six minutes and thirty-two seconds into the call, the caller says, "Oh my God, he's dead." More than nine minutes into the call, a dispatcher asks the caller her name. "Brenda," she says. "Brenda Lazaro."

"When you walked in, what did you see?" the dispatcher asked.

"We were just having a discussion," Lazaro says. "He said he loved me and I didn't believe him and he said this was going prove that he loved me."

As the call wraps up, Wysocki takes the stage. She's wearing a thigh-length tweed blazer over a crisp white shirt and black pants. She's solemn. "You're all going to be Jonathan's voice," she says.

For Wysocki, this isn't a paid speaking engagement. She's here for free and her event, and her collaboration with CrimeCon, is an attempt at activism. The more people who learn about the Crews case, she figures, the better chance it has of being solved. "This is a very important call," Wysocki says. "You're only going to hear it twice. But every time you hear it, you're going to pick up different things." Wysocki never peacocks for the crowd; there's no onstage theatrics. She reminds her attendees that Crews's parents are here and that this is in no way an evening of light, murder-solving fun. "For them," Wysocki says, "this is emotional; it's a grieving and healing process."

Wysocki, herself, has listened to Lazaro's 911 call more than a hundred times since taking the Crews case in late 2014 and she begins to brief the audience on a few of her thoughts. "How many people would be banging on the door, screaming for help," she asks the crowd, "if their significant other was dying?" Then she divides the crowd up into groups, each of which is paired with a PI, who, she says, has traveled here at his or her own expense. There are fourteen of them. Seven are crashing tonight at Wysocki's house. A handful of them will later join Wysocki in launching her second podcast called *Broke, Busted & Disgusted: The Life of American PIs.*

"Everyone's here for one reason, and that's to support the family," says one investigator to his group. He introduces himself to them as Mark Gillespie. Wearing jeans, leather boots, and a navy blazer over a lavender dress shirt, Gillespie looks younger than sixty-one. His almond-brown tan gives him an air of calm; his wife, Cheryl, is standing beside him.

Gillespie and Wysocki met two years ago at a meeting of the Texas Association of Licensed Investigators (TALI) outside of Houston. He was presenting on forensic science; she was in his class, getting information on a few matters critical to the Lauren Agee case, namely, how to analyze bite marks and how unconscious bodies respond to prolonged periods in the water. "She chased me down," Gillespie says, "and we've been friends ever since."

The groups rotate from room to room and in each of the smaller Ryman Studios, satellites surrounding the larger ballroom, there's a display featuring a different aspect of the Crews case. In one, Wysocki has recreated the murder scene. There, a Crews-sized plastic Caucasian male, wearing navy sweats, has been set on its back atop a bed. A sage-colored sheet is pulled up to the dummy's waist. Its shirt is pulled up to its collarbone area revealing a burst of stage blood. On the nightstand next to the bed are several bottles of water and containers of Chinese carryout, mirroring the setup in Crews's bedroom the night he died. There's also a blown-up photograph from the crime scene of Crews's real body: a cop is lifting his shirt while another officer photographs the bullet wound on the left side of his chest, right over his heart.

In other rooms, PIs take attendees through text and Facebook messages from Lazaro and various members of the Crews family. They review information about fingerprints, gunpowder, and bullet trajectory. There's a lot of discussion about the angle at which the bullet went in. If Crews, who was right-handed, had shot himself in the heart while lying in bed, as Lazaro had claimed, that would have meant he had the SIG in his dominant hand, reached across his body, and bent his wrist inward toward his chest to land the fatal shot. It's an unlikely angle to begin with, an unnatural contortion of the wrist, and it's made even more unlikely by a note Wysocki found in Crews's medical file. He had been diagnosed with a shoulder injury by a doctor the day before his death. "Tenderness of Subdeltoid Bursa the Trapezius and the Deltoid," as the medical report indicated, would have made a self-inflicted, cross-body shot difficult to impossible. With an injury like that, Crews may not have been flexible enough to get the gun into position.

Several videos that Wysocki had commissioned were also on view. One showed the violent kickback of the SIG. The gun was found on the bed at the crime scene, but Wysocki and the PIs were positing that the kickback would have likely blown the gun out of Crews's hand and onto the floor.

The fifty-page Coppell Police Department incident report about Crews's death is largely made up of email correspondence from Pam Crews to the detectives investigating her son's case. Her emails are preceded by a short "initial narrative" written by one of the officers at the scene, Aaron Sparks. When he arrived at the Riverchase Apartments, Sparks writes, he was met by Lazaro in front of building 8, where Crews's unit was located. She had blood on the palms of both her hands. She told Sparks she arrived at Crews's home that afternoon, around 4:00 p.m., and that they had been previously arguing, according to the report, "about a girl named Emily." Because of the argument, Lazaro told Sparks she and Crews hadn't spoken to one another for most of the night.

Crews ordered Chinese food at some point (later, when Wysocki interviewed the delivery person, he confessed he'd heard loud arguing on approach to unit 813, disputing Lazaro's account of a mostly silent evening). While Lazaro and Crews ate, the conversation about Emily Tadie was reignited. Lazaro says she was sitting on the floor at the foot of the bed when Crews told her repeatedly to cover her ears and said, "Baby, I love you and I'm going to show you that I love you" (later, according to Pam Crews, Lazaro told her kung fu mentor, Henry Su, that she was in the living room at the time of the gunshot, and not at the foot of the bed; Su denied this in a deposition lasting more than two and a half hours). Lazaro concludes her statement in the "initial narrative" by telling Sparks that Crews "never indicated suicidal tendencies," was sober at the time of his death, and "was always happy." She said she and Crews had been dating about three months. This, she said, was just their third argument.

The next day, February 3, after having been on the scene, Detective Anthony Maurer signed an affidavit saying, "He hereby charges and accuses, that: Brenda Lazaro has committed Murder a violation of Penal Coder 19.02, a felony." In the same affidavit, the SIG is described as a "murder weapon." Further, it says paramedics believed Crews was dead for around thirty minutes when they arrived. They came only ten minutes after Lazaro dialed 911. She had said during the call that he was dying before finally saying he was dead. Had he, in fact, been dead before she even made the call? And why had the murder charge in Maurer's affidavit never become formalized?

In one of her emails to Coppell Police, Pam Crews lays out, at length, what she believes to be the problems with

Lazaro's story. "I realize that you do not have the luxury of having known Jonathan personally," she writes, "to know what is not normal behavior from him."

Near the top of her missive, Pam says her son would never willingly leave his younger brother, Christian, and his younger sister, Dani, behind in this world, not to mention the rest of his family. She takes umbrage with what Lazaro claims were her son's last words. Lazaro told Pam Crews, via Facebook message, that before dying, Jonathan Crews had told her, "Baby, I love you so much, you are my world and I will prove it to you." In the same Facebook message, Lazaro also told Pam Crews: "Jonathan said a lot of nice things to me that night, to the point that I should have known that there was something wrong." That directly conflicts with what Lazaro initially told police: that she and Crews had spent the night silent and upset, fixed in the throes of an ongoing argument.

"Brenda was NOT his world, as she claims he said to her," writes Pam Crews. "He did love her and would have generally liked to have a future with her . . . but he was never fully committed to the relationship because her extreme jealousy, irrationality, and what he described as 'an element of crazy' (which he told me he wanted to watch and see how deep it

ran) kept him at arm's length in terms of a permanent commitment. While he loved her, there were definitely others
that he loved more . . . both friends and family. 'You are my
world,' probably more adequately described Brenda's senti-
ment toward Jonathan than his toward her."

Pam Crews goes on to enumerate all the things that did
fill her son's world. There was his job, where he excelled,
and his commitment to martial arts, which he practiced
with his mom and sister, hoping to improve enough to
join them in their advanced classes. Again, Pam states that
Jonathan would never choose a woman over his family and
friends. "Especially not a woman he was undecided about,
at best, in the first place. He mentioned breaking up with
Brenda (very practically and rationally) to three people on
the same weekend he died. He was not distraught about it."
Pam tells Maurer that Crews had planned upcoming travel:
Colorado in March and Montana, per his custom, in the
summer, to visit his beloved grandfather. He'd been thinking about visiting his brother, too, in India, where he'd be
traveling.

The rest of the email is framed as a series of questions:

If Lazaro said the arguments she and Crews had were
small and resolvable, then why would Crews, stable by all

accounts, need or want to prove his commitment to her in such a dramatic and final way?

Why did it take Lazaro so long to give 911 her exact location? She'd taught kung fu in the area for many years. Wouldn't she know where she was? Was she stalling?

Did Lazaro read through Crews's phone, see his exchanges with Dani and Emily Tadie, and decide, then, to kill him? She had a history of breaking into his Facebook account and even commandeered it after he died, changing his password, and refusing to share it with his siblings. Was she monitoring his texts, too?

If Lazaro was the one who had texted "I want to die" to Tadie, and she did so before Crews was shot, did that, in fact, indicate premeditation? Was this murder in the first degree?

When Crews's iPhone was released back to his family, its screen was badly cracked and its evidence envelope said it was found between his box spring and mattress. Wysocki and Pam Crews both believe Lazaro smashed and hid the phone away after seeing Crews's texts.

Additionally, Pam Crews shares with Maurer her son's extensive history with gun safety. His grandfather, whom Pam calls the most safety-oriented person she's ever known, had taught Crews to shoot from the time he was a boy and had also hired a professional instructor to complete the training. She mentions that the SIG's clip was not in the gun as it had been when Jacob Ramsey had checked it out earlier in the afternoon verifying it as "ready to go." Instead, the clip was found in his tie drawer, which Ramsey cited as strange since, first of all, it wasn't in the gun as it had been earlier, and second, because Crews cared about his appearance and would have never dropped an oiled, lubricated gun clip on top of a row of expensive silk ties.

Who moved the clip, Pam Crews wondered.

And because the gun required five or six pounds of pressure to fire, wouldn't that make it even harder to shoot oneself from Crews's contorted position? That's a heavy trigger, she thought.

Moving from one of her fourteen groups to another, Wysocki encourages the same depth of questioning from her CrimeCon attendees. Being a PI, she says, can largely be about asking everything, of the right sources, at the right time, and for as long as the questions need to be asked.

She passes by an enlarged photograph of Crews's broken phone screen and by the set where she's restaged the murder. She checks in with groups led by Gillespie and by Brandy

Lord, a thirty-nine-year-old PI from Granger, Indiana, with almost twenty years of experience, before moving on to another group led by Chris Yarchuk, a forty-three-year-old detective with Tennessee's White Country Sheriff's Department. Wysocki met Lord at a conference when they were both waiting for a meet and greet with F. Lee Bailey, the famous criminal defense attorney who started his career as a PI, and she met Yarchuk in the earliest days of working the Lauren Agee case. He'd been working at Wakefest as a security officer to make extra money and signaled to Wysocki that the DeKalb County police who were formally handling the case had botched the investigation from the get-go.

Wysocki believes one of the things that sets her apart as an investigator is her national network of other investigators, all from different backgrounds, many with different expertise, from cyber security to kidnappings to forensics. She says that hearing the way her PI friends process and obtain information is invaluable and, in the end, helps her cast a wider investigative net.

Despite setting up her operation as a one-woman business, Wysocki never really works alone. Building such a network, according to many of the PIs I spoke with, is also a shrewd marketing decision. Many of their cases are referrals from their contemporaries.

Jimmie Mesis, a sixty-one-year-old New Jersey–based investigator of four decades, an expert bug sweeper, and the former owner of *PI Magazine*, says the most successful PIs are not former law enforcement officials because they often lack the necessary marketing skills needed to sustain a career on their own. "Former law enforcement have the highest failure rate," he says (he also says they account for 65 percent of the industry). "They have the investigative skills, but can't market to convert it to money," Mesis says. Mesis's figure for the number of PIs in America is slightly higher than the one provided by the Bureau of Labor Statistics (50,000 to their 41,400; 10,000 of the 50,000, he says, are women, who make up the fastest growing demographic in the trade). "There are 250–500 newly licensed PIs in America every month," Mesis says; around the same number of PIs go out of business every four weeks, he continues. According to Mesis, the average life span of a PI agency is just three years and the average age of a PI is between fifty and sixty. Mesis's wife, Roe, sixty-nine, who is also a PI and an instructor, having trained more than 15,000 PIs and having herself tracked down kidnapped children in just hours, says she's seeing more college graduates getting PI licenses and more attorneys getting licensed, too. She sees the profession trending younger as it becomes increasingly digital, too. While the Bureau of Labor Statistics says the 2017 median, annual pay for a PI was $50,700, Mesis says top-tier investigators can make between $250,000 and $500,000 per year.

Before CrimeCon, Wysocki assembled a dossier about the Crews case and made it available to everybody who signed up for her session. It included a summary of events, the emails from Pam Crews to the Coppell Police, and a link to watch Matthew Kirk's deposition. In it, Kirk describes Lazaro showing up at his house the day after Crews died. She asked him whether he'd do anything for her—and then he says she asked if he would kill her.

When Kirk refused, he recalls Lazaro asked him to find her a gun so she could kill herself. Kirk asked Lazaro what had happened, why she was asking to die. She told him her boyfriend had shot himself, not in the heart, but in the head. He pressed her for more information, but she clammed up and left. "I was worried about her," Kirk recalls. "I still kind of liked her."

Pam Crews also recalled Lazaro's extreme neediness in the days after her son's death. After she was questioned by the police at the station, let go, and picked up by Henry Su, Lazaro clung to the Crews family for a few days (she later went back to Jonathan Crews's apartment and spent some time there alone). Pam Crews remembers, despite being in mourning along with her husband and her two other children, that she had to attend to Lazaro—whom her son had been dating for about three months—more than anybody. Around the second week in February, things began to turn between Lazaro and the Crewses. Lazaro and Crews's siblings had issues in regards to his Facebook page: who controlled it and which friends were posting and leaving memorial tributes. Lazaro asked Dani Crews if her brother had told her about Lazaro's past and in other messages she repeatedly said Crews's death was her fault. "I feel responsible for his dead," she wrote. "All this was my fault."

Lazaro didn't show up for Crews's memorial service or his funeral, where the Crewses had saved her a seat in a place of honor with the family, and conveyed to Dani that she was taken aback by not being asked to be more centrally involved in the ceremony. She was stung that Crews's parents did not ask her to deliver a eulogy.

"You can't fault them," Dani Crews wrote. "They just lost their first-born son."

"If they had time to included all his best friends, why didn't they have time to include me?" Lazaro responded.

Looking through the Facebook message exchange between Lazaro and Dani Crews, it's hard to look away from their avatars. Dani posted a photograph of her brother Jonathan, with her leaning into him; his arm wraps around her, bringing her close in the manner of a protector. Lazaro's photo, on the other hand, shows her and Crews lying down, possibly in the bed where he died, their bodies entangled, their lips locked.

"They wanted you to sit with us," Dani Crews wrote back. "We saved you a seat."

"Really? Just a seat?" Lazaro responded. "So I don't talk and say the true about what really happened? So I don't say how traumatic was his last minutes of life and I had to see and live all that with him. Which I'm really happy I was the last person he saw because I know how much I meant for him, but is not fair at all that you all left me out of his life and try to comfort me by saving a seat for me."

"I needed you there," Dani Crews wrote to Lazaro, whom she also referred to as her best friend. "It's hard for everyone. My mother had been sedated for a week. He was the only member of my family that made me feel like I mattered."

"I understand that Dani," Lazaro wrote, "but he was my only reason of life."

WHEN WYSOCKI ARRIVED IN Coppell, Texas, in November 2014, she started her process of interviewing about eighty people for the case at the Wu Yi Shaolin Martial Arts Center. She had a list from Pam Crews of everybody Jonathan ever knew or who might have known him. Wysocki sat outside and just watched the school for a few hours: who came in and out, how people moved, whom they talked to. She studied body language and looked for any suspicious tics or patterns. They next day she enrolled in a tai chi class, telling Henry Su she was running a nonprofit women's self-defense group and she wanted to see if Wu Yi would be a good place to send people for classes (Wysocki is technically the head of such of a nonprofit group). While taking tai chi herself, Wysocki saw Dani Crews, who didn't know the inflexible newcomer having trouble with the motions was investigating her brother's death. Wysocki also carefully watched Brenda Lazaro and found it peculiar how people always surrounded her in between breaks in the action, as if they were circling to protect somebody who had been hurt.

One of the people surrounding Lazaro was her husband. She got married in 2015. Wysocki says when she got a good look at Lazaro's eyes, she was struck by their coloring. "They were very dark," Wysocki says. "Very dark. I mean, dark." Wysocki says the martial arts studio reminded her of a cult for the way its members kept talking about it like a family. Pam and Dani Crews stopped taking classes there.

Outside of the studio, Wysocki tracked down Karen Petree, a close friend of Lazaro's, at the high school where Petree taught French. Lazaro had shown up at Petree's house not long after Crews died and the two women had also taken a camping trip alone in the spring of 2014, just a few months after the incident, to Kickapoo Cavern State Park, almost 400 miles southwest of Coppell. "Girlfriends tell one another things," Wysocki told me. "Period." She figured Lazaro may have confessed to Petree outright, or maybe have at least relayed important information about the events leading up Crews's death. Wysocki's questioning of Petree helped set Tom Shaw up to depose her over the course of 103 minutes on April 28, 2016.

During the deposition, Petree, thirty-one, with her brown hair pulled back and wearing a white sleeveless blouse and silver teardrop earrings, reveals that she had likely last spoken to Lazaro about a month before at her baby shower and that Lazaro had recently given birth. The two women, at the time of the deposition, had been friends for over a decade; they met at the kung fu school, which Petree also says was like a family. For almost two hours, however, Petree answers questions in a manner that alternatingly suggests a close relationship with Lazaro and very little concern for Lazaro at all. She knows all about Lazaro witnessing a murder as a kid in Mexico, but also says she knew very little about Matthew Kirk, whom Lazaro had dated for four years, and says she had never met Crews.

When Shaw asks Petree about what she knew of Crews, she said, "A lot went in one ear and out the other." When Shaw asks Petree if she feels more aligned with Lazaro and her legal team than she does with him, she says, "Well, yeah."

Petree says that Lazaro and Crews were talking about getting married, but, also, that she and Lazaro never once spoke about Crews during their two-woman sojourn to Kickapoo Cavern. The end of the deposition mostly shows Petree flip-flopping over whether or not she had heard from Lazaro that Crews intended to end their relationship.

Shaw, at one point, asks Petree why her friend would take the Fifth in her own deposition if she were merely innocent?

Wysocki tells me Lazaro took the Fifth 128 times during questioning so as not to incriminate herself.

Another investigative step took Wysocki to the Coppell Fire Department to talk to the emergency medical responders who were summoned to Crews's apartment the night he died. One EMS worker told Wysocki how to file the proper information requests to obtain their reports. Wysocki, however, decided that that wasn't the result she wanted, so she planted herself in a chair, sitting for over an hour and making intermittent comments. The EMS worker ultimately made copies of the relevant reports for Wysocki and told her he couldn't just give them to her while placing them down on a table and making it clear he was turning his back so she could take the documents and leave. Wysocki also asked him to recall what he could about his ambulance run to the Crews apartment. "He explained that Jonathan's body wasn't the body of somebody who had just died," Wysocki says. "Too cold, too much blood." Wysocki remembers the medical tech saying that it didn't look like a suicide.

Further, he warned Wysocki that the Coppell PD could be sloppy around crime scenes. Indeed, she says they moved the SIG and failed to photograph it where it was found; they didn't take fingerprints on the gun either, claiming it wouldn't matter because so many people had touched it in recent days, including Ramsey. Wysocki has since consulted with homicide detectives independent of the Coppell PD, asking whether their too-many-fingerprints theory holds any water. "That's what cops say when they know they didn't do their job," a Houston-based detective told Wysocki. One of the PIs working with Wysocki at Crime-Con had a term for the phenomenon of a police department rallying around one of its own to bury critical errors. "It's called the blue wall, cops will defend each other" said the PI. "The police don't like us going back over their work," Wysocki, says.

Regardless, Wysocki knew she had to show up at Coppell police headquarters. She asked John Crews to set up a formal appointment, a courtesy she extends to other law enforcement professionals, thinking the cops would be more likely to respond to the father of the deceased rather than to her. John Crews, Wysocki says, didn't want much to do with her in the early days of her investigation. He wasn't opposed to her services and even believed them to be necessary, but she also directly represented Jonathan's tragic absence. "He couldn't sit in the same room as me," Wysocki says. "You could see the pain in his face."

Along with Chris Hawkins, a thirty-six-year-old PI whose license she works under in Texas, Wysocki walked into the Coppell Police Department intent on meeting the detective working the case. Wysocki was told by a secretary that the detective would not be available; Wysocki asked if another detective could take the meeting instead. No, the secretary said. Wysocki asked for a sergeant. No sergeants, the woman said. "Well," said Wysocki, "how about the chief of police?" Another secretary emerged and told Wysocki that all the people she had asked to talk to weren't in the building. "They're all at burglary," the secretary said. "So rude," Wysocki says. "I'm used to being told to leave places, to being thrown out, but to treat a family like this is beyond me. They treat Pam like she's a crazy mom who can't accept things." Within thirty minutes, Wysocki remembers getting a call from the original detective with whom she requested a meeting. He told her that unless Lazaro confesses, they have nothing.

At nearly 11:00 p.m., Wysocki's fourteen groups reunite as one in the Ryman Ballroom to ask her questions. From the stage, she tells her audience that she hopes their night of sleuthy group-think will change the case. It's Wysocki's belief that one thing that has a good chance of injecting life into a lifeless-seeming case is participation. A critical mass tasked with a problem, she believes, is hard thing to stop. The questions asked are well-formed and intelligent. They cover Lazaro's 911 call and the difficulty of Crews being able to shoot himself at such an angle with such a gun. The most jarring questions are the ones for Pam and John Crews, who have taken the stage with Wysocki.

One woman asks Pam Crews for some details to "humanize Jonathan." She says the whole night has been about his death and that some testimony about his life would be appreciated. At first, it seems like an awful thing to ask. A stranger intrusively asking a mother to remember. But the way Pam Crews answers the question also illuminates that its real motivation is kindness. Pam tells a story about Jonathan flushing his father's watch down the toilet as a boy and then another story about a young Jonathan earnestly looking for ways to cure AIDS. Telling the story of who Jonathan was, Wysocki says, might also drive the case to a conclusion. A wave of goodness seems to wash over the room. "Everyone here is here to help," Wysocki tells me later.

Since the Coppell Police say there isn't substantial evidence to mount a criminal case against Lazaro—despite, says Wysocki, finding gun powder residue on both of her hands—the Crews family filed a civil complaint against Lazaro in the form of wrongful death suit. Trial was set for July 2018, then moved to November 2018. But a couple weeks before the trial date, the Crews family had gone to court asking for a continuance and a later trial as Wysocki and her team would soon have new evidence they would need to analyze and process. A new trial date was set for April before another postponement (At the time this book went to press, Wysocki, Shaw, and the Crews family were awaiting a new trial date.)

Upon the conclusion of CrimeCon, Wysocki continued to investigate the case. Some of the people who had enrolled in her session also continued to discuss it on a Facebook page dedicated to it and one of them suggested Lazaro, whose Spanish interfered with her English diction and grammar, was speaking Spanish at one point during the 911 call. Wysocki made a note to see if she could have an audio engineer isolate anything said in a foreign language. She also kept on trying to retrieve all of Lazaro's phone and social media records, but AT&T, who held her phone data, and Facebook, where Lazaro communicated regularly, were not cooperating with the subpoenas Crews's team had filed.

There was also the matter of whether the Coppell Police had interviewed Lazaro at the station on the night of Crews's death. Wysocki wonders about the whereabouts of that recording. "Can you imagine what's in those tapes?" Wysocki says.

In October 2018, Wysocki was attending a financial conference in Las Vegas with her husband and sons. "Charles wants us all to learn more about investing," she says. Bored with the material, she noticed a legal conference happening across the hall, at which Wysocki just started looking for resources for her caseload. There, she met representatives from a forensics lab who would be able to determine the height of whoever shot Jonathan Crews based on his wound pattern and the bullet's trajectory. When Tom Shaw heard about this development, he and Wysocki immediately decided it could lead to an investigative breakthrough and that Wysocki would fly to the forensics lab in Pennsylvania to see if the bullet, beyond a shadow of a doubt, was fired by someone standing over Jonathan Crews and not by his own contorted hand.

Wysocki also wrangled the use of a Faro 3D laser scanner, a costly device whose four models range in price from $23,500 to $67,000. The scanner can capture millions of data points at a crime scene. She planned to use it to restage Crews's murder yet again, hoping that the addition of newly acquired technology would lead to firmer conclusions about bullet trajectory and gun discharge residue patterns, and finally answer the question about who shot Jonathan Crews.

Wysocki says if her new evidence presents a substantial breakthrough, a criminal trial might happen after all.

At the time this book went to press in March 2019, no criminal charges had been filed against Lazaro. Wysocki was working to produce new evidence for the upcoming civil trial. A spokesperson from the Coppell Police Department said their own investigation was currently inactive. "But," he added, "it doesn't mean that the case is closed. It just simply means we haven't received any new information. If we do receive new information then it is reactivated."

A FEW WEEKS AFTER CrimeCon, Wysocki invites me to visit her home in Nashville where she's ordered trays of Costco sandwiches and cut fruit in case anybody gets hun-

gry. Her puppy, Niko, a Pomeranian-husky mix, keeps paw-
ing at my lap while Bell, her Chihuahua, lazes indifferently
in her heated doggie bed. (Wysocki points out she bought
it on sale and rarely pays full retail price for anything; she'll
later attempt to negotiate a better price on a Faro 3D laser
scanner she'll share with Gillespie.) "I don't know what's
up with Niko," Wysocki says. "She usually doesn't do this
with people." Wysocki gets Niko to settle down after briefly
playing tug-of-war with a stuffed llama and then looks at
her to-do list, which lays out 105 different tasks.

She'll go check on her mother in the assisted living community where she lives, pick up her mail at a place called
Going Postal (Wysocki uses a PO box rather than her home
address), and she'll also interview a potential intern at a
Starbucks in nearby Murfreesboro.

The first question Wysocki will ask the female college
student is, "How do you feel about investigating the case of
a girl your age who was killed?" Her follow-up: "If I have
autopsy photographs, they peel the skin off the person—
you all right with that?"

"You're not afraid of conflict?" Wysocki asks.

She asks her applicant if she's prepared to face the kind
of sexism Wysocki herself has dealt with throughout her

career and tells her she's currently mentoring four female PIs around the country. "As a woman getting into this situation," she says, "we're considered bitches. 'Oh, here comes the bitch. She's a bully. She's crazy.'"

Another to-do is a visit from a security professional and a friend of Wysocki's named David Gray, who is on his way over to check for any bugs on Wysocki's phones and computers. Wysocki says that one day, while she was working on Lauren Agee's case, her computer's cursor just started moving around the screen. She wasn't controlling it. Whoever was began clicking open her files. Ever since then, Gray has come by at least once a month to sweep for bugs and make sure no outside parties have access to Wysocki's electronic files or can listen to her in her home from a remote location.

While Gray conducts his sweep, waving a small electronic device over an array of other surfaces, I sit in Wysocki's living room with Sherry Smith, whose daughter, Lauren Agee, died on July 26, 2015. Smith is wearing a tan skirt, a few shades lighter than her tan skin. Her hair is up. The gold insignias on her Tory Burch sandals glimmer. Her pedicure includes a small flower painted on her big toe. On Smith's wrist is a bracelet featuring a series of angel wings. She looks at the wings while explaining how difficult it has been for her to keep it together over the years, without Lauren, always wondering what happened to her. Smith says she's had panic attacks on many a night. But she feels she owes it to her daughter to keep searching for the truth. "Lauren was loud," Smith says, "big personality, filled up every room. Every time I get down, I can just hear her saying, '*Mom!*' 'And I snap right to.'"

Wysocki took on Lauren Agee's case in early 2016. Agee had died the previous summer while camping on Center Hill Lake during a wakeboarding festival. Her campsite was on a cliff. Getting there required a canoe and a steep climb. Agee camped with her childhood friend, Hannah Palmer, Palmer's new boyfriend, Aaron Lilly, and two friends of Lilly's, Chris Stout and Heydrich Brixner Gambrell, who goes by his nickname, Brix.

The weekend, by witness accounts, was steeped in post-adolescent drama and chaos. The campers got sloppy drunk. Issues between ex-boyfriends and ex-girlfriends manifested into confrontations.

Around 5:00 p.m. on a Sunday, Lauren Agee's body was found floating in the water. Agee was petite, five feet four, and 118 pounds. The people who discovered her thought they had discovered a dead child. Her friends, who said they last saw her at 3:00 a.m., went out for the whole day without her, and without contact from her, and didn't find that odd enough to report her missing.

When the police arrived, they failed to secure the crime scene. Some of Agee's possessions vanished and were never returned to Smith. The campers were questioned, gave written statements—Aaron Lilly spells his own name incorrectly in his; Chris Stout refers to Agee as "the girl," and not by her name—and were told they could go home by around 7:00 p.m.

Smith and her husband, Michael, Lauren's stepfather, were met at the hospital by a DeKalb County detective named Jeremy Taylor. Smith says Taylor told her Lauren's head was split open like a watermelon (which was not the case) and they weren't allowed to see the body. From the beginning, Smith says, DeKalb County law enforcement treated her and her husband as if they were the ones breaking the law. "Like we were criminals," Smith says, "like we were bothering them, like we were crazy, like, 'Ma'am you just need to let me do my job, go away.'"

Jeremy Taylor closed his investigation on September 23, 2015, about three months after Agee's death. His memo closing the case consists of three short paragraphs. In them, Taylor says he'd found no foul play, but he doesn't show much in the way of police work either. Taylor determined that Agee fell from the cliff. No one was arrested and no charges were brought against anyone in connection with the death.

The medical examiner ruled cause of death as "blunt trauma to head and back." "Possible drowning "was listed as the "contributory cause of death." The manner of death, according to the medical examiner, was an accident.

Not satisfied with the brevity, insensitivity, inaccuracy, and incomplete nature of Taylor's investigation, Smith eventually found her way to Wysocki through a friend claiming to have psychic powers. The friend had seen Wysocki in the press and had a feeling she was the one to bring justice to the family. "There's always a psychic at some point," Wysocki told me.

Once she took over the case, Wysocki began going back over everything. She visited the campsite on multiple occasions and climbed the cliff despite a fear of both heights and snakes. She procured a dummy about the size of Lauren Agee's body and had it thrown from the cliff repeatedly to see how it might fall and where it might land. While Agee's body was bruised, Wysocki thinks she'd have been far more cut up had she abruptly fallen. The drop was neither sheer nor unobstructed. Agee's body wouldn't have plummeted so much as tumbled violently downward.

Wysocki also hired a hydrologist to study how and in which direction Agee's body would have floated over a certain period of time. And she had her autopsy reevaluated. The original report says the face shows minor injuries, but a photo shows her nose is clearly broken. There's a line in the report about a tampon found in Agee's vagina, which Smith finds suspect since she says she knew "Lauren was not on her period. I'm her mom. I know those things."

Taylor had also told Agee's father and stepfather that their daughter could not have been raped because that tampon was in; no rape kit was conducted.

The medical examiner listed that there were no injuries to the throat, but Wysocki had a photograph of the throat studied and says there's evidence of strangling. Wysocki soon tracked down Lilly and Hannah Palmer in Florida, where they had moved shortly after Wakefest, gotten married, and had a child. During her conversation with Palmer, Lilly, who was not home, calls repeatedly.

While Palmer and Wysocki spoke in the living room, Gambrell kept nervously entering the kitchen and exiting through a back door. Eventually Lilly came home. "I've only felt in the presence of pure evil a couple of times during my career," Wysocki says. "This was one of those times." Having taped all of it, Wysocki included the conversation in her pod-cast about Agee's case, which debuted in the fall of 2018 and al-most immediately entered the top 100 podcasts on iTunes. In the months since, Wysocki has released twenty-two episodes.

When I first met with Sherry Smith, in May 2018, she believed the podcast might be her best shot at justice. She feared, after three years of grieving and investigating, that a trial against the other campers might never materialize. Smith recalls leaving court dejected after one particular pro-ceeding to see whether charges could be pressed against Han-nah Palmer. A DeKalb county judge ruled they could not.

"People are offended that Sheila's a woman," Smith says. "Especially in the South. They really are. They are offended that she is also a mom, and this judge, when we're done pre-senting all of our information in regard to summary judg-ment for Hannah, the judge started reprimanding all of us for wasting his time, and my attorney for wasting my money. And he looks at Sheila and he goes, 'And you don't even have a college education.'"

Smith points out that Jeremy Taylor, the detective who had investigated her daughter's case, didn't even finish high school. She found this out after Wysocki had asked to sub-poena his employee file.

In September 2018, Wysocki removed herself from the Agee case as its PI on the same day the Smiths dropped their wrongful death lawsuit against the campers. Sherry was fearful that a gag order issued by a judge would result in her going to jail. Wysocki, having resigned as the case's PI, said she'd continue working on it through her podcast as an investigative journalist. "We're getting closer to the killer," Wysocki says. "I might never take on another case without also doing a podcast about it."

Meanwhile, prior to dropping the case, Smith had taken it to the Tennessee state court of appeals in Nashville, and in January 2019, they ruled in her favor, opening the case back up to further proceedings. Wysocki says Smith's first action now is to try and get the case removed from DeKalb County so it can be heard without bias.

IN THE DINING ROOM, Wysocki and Gray, having completed their debugging, are on the phone with a confidential source who worked as a 911 dispatcher in Coppell, Texas. Niko is sleeping beneath the table and Wysocki is gathering background on what callers sound like when they dial in after or during an emergency.

Did Lazaro fit any pattern? What did her tone suggest? Was she stalling? Did she sound consistent with other reports of suicide? Or did her behavior signal something else? And what did this dispatcher, who did not handle Lazaro's call, think of it all? Wysocki also wanted to know if the operators asked the right questions of Lazaro. Did they elicit information in the most efficient way? Did they get in the way of the truth? Wysocki took notes. She asked her questions openly and kindly. The point was clearly to know everything. To leave nothing up in the air. To ask questions until all the answers were gathered and understood.

Smith noted Wysocki's diligence.

"She's going to solve my daughter's death," she said. "I know it."

ACKNOWLEDGMENTS

The author would like to extend a special thanks to:

Sheila Wysocki, Charles Wysocki, Mark Gillespie, Cheryl Gillespie, Tom Shaw, John and Pam Crews, Sherry and Michael Smith, Brandy Lord, Madison Gabbard, Kelly Riddle, Mike Kenny, David Gray, Jimmie Mesis, Roe Mesis, Steven Rambam, Liz Greenwood, David Zeldin, Tom Ruskin, Kevin Balfe, Becky Drumwright, David Gray, Troy Flemming, Jay Marin, George Gergis, Chris Yarchuk, Chris Hawkins, Greg Shaffer, Kevin Walters, Jim Rutman, Karyn Marcus, Max Meltzer, Molly Gregory, Phil Metcalf, Alexis Minieri, Allison Har-zvi, Alex French, Luke Zaleski, Dan Martensen, and John Pelosi.

ABOUT THE AUTHOR

Howie Kahn is a contributing editor for *WSJ. The Wall Street Journal Magazine*; founding host of *Prince Street*, a food and culture podcast heard in more than 200 countries; and coauthor of the *New York Times* bestseller *Sneakers*. His work, on an array of topics—from demolition workers in Detroit to social and environmental justice pioneers in Texas and Wyoming, has appeared in more than three dozen publications, including *GQ*, *Wired*, *Elle*, and *O: The Oprah Magazine*. Kahn is the winner of a James Beard Award for food feature writing and a graduate of the University of Michigan and the Sarah Lawrence College MFA program.